Twany Beckham

Pressure

PRESSURE

Written by: Twany Beckham

Cover Art by: George Daugherty

Edited by: Terri Bradshaw and Andrew Clark

ISBN: 9781728622101

Copyright © 2018 by Twany Beckham

All rights reserved. No parts of this book shall be reproduced, stored in a retrieval system, or transmitted by any means, electronic, mechanical, photocopying, recording, or otherwise, without written permission from the author and publisher.

Published by ONE DREAM GROUP, LLC

Twany Beckham

I dedicate this book to anyone in the world who needs motivation to overcome adversity and the pressures of life. I also dedicate this book to my step dad, Andre Gardner Sr. and Aunty, Angela Thomas, who were both called to heaven way too soon!

Pressure

God will never leave you empty handed. He will replace everything that you've lost. If he asks you to put something down, it's because he wants you to pick up something greater.

-Unknown

"Trust in the lord with all your hearts, and lean not on your own understanding. In all your way acknowledge him, and he will make your path straight."

-Proverbs 3:5-6

Twany Beckham

PRESSURE is a read about overcoming adversity and appreciating opportunities in the face of all pressures. I am a young man who has embarked on an unimaginable journey and I have learned a lot. With all that I have learned, I wish to share and pay it forward.

I've been fortunate to take the pressures of life and turn them into self-discovery and Pure JOY. As we all know, everyone has a different story but the principles in which we conquer pressures are all similar.

In this book, I have captured the pressures of many others to show that we are all capable of overcoming any pressure that God places in our lives.

Where are you in your life? Are you living in your dreams? Are you living with purpose? Are you experiencing real JOY?

Has adversity struck in your life? If so, how are you handling it? Or, how did you handle it? Are you fighting to redefine your life? Are you vying for inner peace?

Wherever you are, I can relate. I've been there, on all ends of the spectrum. I still fight for peace every day. It's a constant battle.

Pressure

No matter where life has taken you, this book was meant for you.

EMBRACE THE JOURNEY

George Raveling
www.coachgeorgeraveling.com

Each of us must be on a personal journey to find something in life that emotionally connects and inspires our spirit. Do not wait until you are older to become wiser. Do not expect to be chosen. Choose yourself every single day. Transfer your mind from a fixed mindset to a growth mindset.

Each day perform like your life depends on it while not allowing the opinions of others to drown out your inner voice. Success is "continuously improving who you are, how you live, how you serve and how you relate." Learn to accept, embrace and make peace with life's many changes and challenges. This transcending act alone will make life easier, allowing us to become wiser in the discovery.

Residing in your comfort zone lessens the chances of something remarkable, magical, and the impossible from happening. Mind management is much more crucial than time management. Learning to conquer your doubts and fears is the beginning of everlasting transformation and sustainable growth.

Unfortunately, many of us give up our curiosity too soon. You are not your failures. You are not

Pressure

your past. Small actions compound. Every successful person I have encountered had a perseverance story to share. The obstacle is the way. There will always be light at the end of the lesson. You have to stay the course. Keep searching and persevering. What stands in the way becomes the way!

Table of Contents

Foreword: Written by Max Appel

Chapter 1: Featuring Debra Beckham...................1-9

Interlude: Featuring Christopher Gowers..........10-15

Chapter 2: Featuring Eric Dean Tooley................16-23

Chapter 3: Featuring Andre Gardner and Stan Whitaker..24-45

Chapter 4: Featuring Jamal Crook...................46-61

Chapter 5: Featuring NyRee Clayton-Taylor......62-72

Chapter 6: Featuring Deanna Boone................73-85

Interlude Two:..86-89

Chapter 7: Featuring Kyle Wiltjer and Jazzmar Ferguson...90-106

Chapter 8: Featuring Asia Poore and Sydney Poore 107-121

Chapter 9: Featuring Corey Shane Taylor......122-133

Chapter 10: Featuring Katherine Hanly and Holly Simmons..134-149

Pressure

Chapter 11: Featuring Phil Fowler and Chris Hudson..150-163

Chapter 12:......................................…..164-167

Acknowledgements: Featuring Rev. Willis Polk ....…..168-172

Interlude Three: Featuring Kobe Bryant and Inky Johnson...173-178

Contact Author:...179

*All featured interviews were conducted, transcribed, and edited by the Author.

Twany Beckham

Foreword by Max Appel

When Twany asked me to write about life being a journey with pressures we face along the way, I thought about how his life reflected the lines from a Robert Frost poem.

"Two roads diverged in a wood, and I - I took the one less traveled by, and that has made all the difference."

While many people succumb to the fear that often accompanies pressure, Twany not only confronted these pressures, he learned valuable life-lessons from them and grew as a person and as a Christ-follower.

Life is a journey and I believe the joy is in the journey. We often focus on our destination, but it is the highs and the lows we encounter along the way that help shape us into the people we are today. To quote the famous Dr. Seuss from his book "Oh, The Places You'll Go",

"You have brains in your head.
You have feet in your shoes.
You can steer yourself any direction you choose.
You're on your own.
And you know what you know.

Pressure

And YOU are the guy who'll decide where to go.

...And will you succeed?
Yes! You will indeed!
(98 and 3/4 percent guaranteed)"

We will face trials and tribulations on our journey - valleys of disappointment and rivers of loneliness. We will also have mountain-top experiences with success, laughter, and meet wonderful people who cross our path. Twany's persistence encourages us, in spite of pressure, to not miss the journey! Don't be a spectator, don't just stand on the sidelines, get in the game. This game called life. Our 26th President of the United States, Theodore Roosevelt, puts it this way:

"It is not the critic who counts; not the man who points out how the strong man stumbles, or where the doer of deeds could have done them better. The credit belongs to the man who is actually in the arena, whose face is marred by dust and sweat and blood; who strives valiantly; who errs, who comes short again and again, because there is no effort without error in shortcoming; but who does actually strive to do the deeds; who knows great enthusiasms, the great devotions; who spends himself in a worthy cause; who at the best knows in

Twany Beckham

the end the triumph of high achievement, and who at the worst, if he fails, at least fails while daring greatly, so that his place shall never be with those cold and timid souls who neither know victory nor defeat."

Dream! And then dream some more! And then turn your dreams into a reality. Do not allow the pressures of life to rob you of your identity or your purpose. Do not leave with your song unsung. When the pressures come, and they will, choose faith over fear. I've seen this work in Twany's life and I know it will also work for you. Michael Card, a Christian songwriter, penned these words in his song, "Joy in the Journey".

"There is a joy in the journey,
there's a light we can love on the way.
There is a wonder and wildness to life,
and freedom for those who obey.
All those who seek it shall find it,
a pardon for all who believe.
Hope for the hopeless and sight for the blind
to all who've been born of the Spirit. . ."

My life verses in the Bible are Proverbs 3:5-6 - "Trust in the Lord with all your heart and lean not on your own understanding; in all your ways acknowledge Him, and He will make your paths straight." Follow

Pressure

this advice and oh, the places you will go!

PRESSURE can kill you……………………

However, the context in this book will exemplify how PRESSURE can also make you one of the strongest individuals in the world….

Pressure

Chapter 1

As the commissioner of the National Basketball Association (NBA) walked to the podium to announce the last pick of the 2013 NBA draft, my television went into slow motion mode. After having back surgery, which essentially ended my basketball career, I still had an illusion that my name was going to be called on NBA draft night. Yes... I endured the pain of false hope. The 2013 NBA draft was the longest three hours of my life.

I spent 24 years of my life chasing a dream that I came close to reaching. I did everything in my willpower to make this dream a reality. I put my mind and body through hell. My mother sacrificed many years of her life to allow me the opportunities to chase my dreams and for it to end so fast was devastating.

As the Memphis Grizzlies selected their player with the 60th pick, life changed for me instantly.

I did not hear my name called as a draft pick.
The foresight of using basketball to become a multi-millionaire to provide a better life for my family shred to pieces.

I was heartbroken.
My spirits were crushed.

I knew beforehand that the odds of me being drafted were 0.00% so I don't even know why I watched the draft. I was used to experiencing pain, so to me, this was just another instance...that I thought would be easily shakable. I sat silently and watched the past 24 years of my life disintegrate in three hours.

I didn't have much time to recover. Life kept on doing what it does best...moving right along. My thoughts immediately pondered around what 9-5 jobs I was going to start applying for... something you never think about, especially while playing college basketball at the highest level.

I thought about my family back at home, who were still in the routine of struggling. I struggled with realizing that I wasn't going to be able to make a difference...well, not at that particular moment at least. On top of worrying about everyone in the struggle, I now had to make sure I didn't fall back victim to it.

Monthly bills and everything associated with adulthood were about to smack me right in the face.

Pressure

Where was I going to live? How was I going to put food on the table? What other dreams could I pursue now that basketball was over?
I had to start life completely over. I was twenty-five years old with no idea what I wanted to do for the rest of my life. Growing up, I never pictured life without basketball. I never imagined waking up without the ability to lace up my sneakers to go play the game I love. I understood that this day would eventually creep into my reality, but just not at twenty-five. I was still young with a lot left in the tank.

I was walking into a new life of PRESSURE. Living the good college life and playing at one of the best programs in the country was over. There was no more Kentucky basketball. There were no more private flights around the country, free Nike gear, training table, or Head Coach John Calipari.

I battled heavily with trusting others. Once the news spread that my basketball career was over, many of my friendships ended. Praise to God...I kept my sanity. There was no one to turn to...no one I felt like I could trust to keep my pain in secrecy. It was hard finding outlets for all of my thoughts.

Twany Beckham

I made my mind up to fight through the tough times and stand strong through all the highs and lows.

I was on my own now in this crazy world with the pressure of making something of myself all over again, but I knew that I could because I BELIEVED that I could.

My mother would always tell me that the weak never make it out of where we grew up and that she knew I would bounce back from my failures.

My recovery after the final game of my high school career was the epitome of what my mother meant by telling me that I would bounce back from all of my failures.

In the biggest basketball game of my life, I played the worst game imaginable. With a state championship on the line and 24,000 fans in attendance, I laid an egg. I was one of the best players in the state of Kentucky and only made one basket in the State Championship game. I could blame the referees for the horrible fouls called, that sat me for the majority of the game. But in life, there are no excuses. Scrutiny that would've torn many to pieces fueled me and what I stood for. A situation many would've looked at as a

Pressure

failure was a learning experience that will stick with me forever.
It made me fearless.

I have experienced a feeling that I never thought I would experience. I did something that a lot of us fail to have the opportunity of doing.

I lived my dreams.

If you grew up in Kentucky and played basketball, you dreamed of playing college ball at either the University of Louisville or the University of Kentucky.

My dream was always to play at Kentucky and as hard as this dream was to conquer, I did it. On top of putting that jersey on that read KENTUCKY across the chest, I also got to play with future NBA superstars.

Winning a National Championship in 2012 was one of the greatest moments of my life, that I will always be grateful for.

As I've grown into the man I am today, having gone through so many obstacles to achieve success, I've learned to never blame the deck of cards that were stacked up against me, but appreciate every little hindrance that I've encountered. Blaming anything or anyone for not achieving success and being joyful in life wasn't something that I could ever be comfortable doing.

Life for me hasn't been all peaches and cream and I could have easily folded under pressure under some circumstances.

Where should I start, let's see.... born to a single mother with little to no education who lived in one of the worst projects in Louisville, Kentucky. By the time I turned three years of age, I had two little brothers and we never consistently had a father figure in our home. We have had the windows of our house flooded with bullets. We have had close friends and family members murdered. We have also experienced the feeling of being homeless.

Hard times has always managed to lay its nest near our family but the checkered flag, has never been waved

As I've brought you into my life a little... I want you to think about the odds that were stacked up against me and the likelihood of me being successful.

Based on the negative statistics of kids born into poverty, many would say my chances weren't very high. Now, even though the measuring stick for success is different for every individual, I've always viewed success in the light of someone from my neighborhood who graduated from college.

You're probably shaking your head thinking to yourself, how in the world did this kid make it? How did his mother manage to raise three boys without any significant help from a male figure, or your mind is probably wondering, where is all this leading to? No matter where your thoughts lie, I just hope you haven't felt any urge to feel sorry for me.

All that I want you to feel and think about is the amount of pressure that was placed on a single mother and three young boys. I also want you to know that we can overcome anything, if we put our minds to it.

Pressure made me who I am

Debra Beckham

It was extremely hard raising three boys as a single mother living in the projects. I struggled to maintain stable relationships with either of their fathers so that made it that much harder. I felt like I had to do everything for my boys on my own. You had to do what you had to do just to survive each and every day. Life isn't about where you live; it's about how you live. When my boys were first born, I didn't really work a lot and assistance from the government was mediocre. I did receive food stamps every month and that really helped out a lot. It helped me keep food on the table. When the boys got a little older, I went back to work and was working two to three jobs just to make ends meet and to support my family. I started out working in restaurants where I served for many years. Then I got into working in the warehouse industry and that's where I stayed as my kids grew up. Working in the warehouse industry was hard for many years, especially the jobs where I had to stand on my feet day in and day out but I did what I had to do.

The pressure of raising my kids was simply to give them a better life and making sure that I got them out of the projects. I tried my best to make sure that they didn't get caught up in the gangs, doing drugs, stealing, getting into trouble amongst several things that could have been presented. Gun violence was always a scare and I prayed every day that my kids made it home at night.

My kids were always good kids. They listened to me. I was very strict on them. They got into

Pressure

trouble every now and then but it was never anything serious. I never really had doubts about my kids making it out because I had a strong mind and I was determined to do everything that I possibly could for them. Once I had my mind set that they were going to be successful then I stuck with it. There were times where we really struggled financially but I was determined to never let my kids know about it. I had a pretty good childhood but once I got around that 15/16 mark, I went buck wild and got myself in trouble here and there. I went through some things as an early adult that I never wanted to see my kids go through so that always kept me motivated. I didn't want to them taking the road that I took in life.

I am very satisfied with the job that I did raising my kids. I am proud of where they all are in their lives and I know it's only going to continue to get better. I wouldn't change anything about the way I raised my kids and where I raised them. I think the projects definitely made my boys tough and who they are.

I am Debra Beckham and I have survived PRESSURE.

Interlude

In a society filled with relationships that struggle to meet common generosity and people befriending others because of specific needs, I have been fortunate to befriend several people who I know will be by my side through any pressures. One of those friends is Chris Gowers. Friends like Chris do not come along often.

Chris and I grew up very differently, yet he is like a brother to me. When we first met, he didn't look at me any different because of where I came from. He and his family accepted my friends and me as if we were family. Our relationship continues to only get stronger the older we get.

Pressure made me who I am

Chris Gowers

Growing up, it was me, my sister and both of our parents. My parents were my framework. They were the first example that I saw of what a mother and a father were supposed to look like.

Our initial structure was always about family and open communication. My dad was a businessman and my mom was a stay at home mom. Having my mom at home was really beneficial to my sister and I. Anything we needed at school, she was there. If we were hungry, she was cooking. My dad was always traveling for work. He was the epitome of how dedication and hard work brought one success. To me, they both were the best at the roles that they played.

My mom's family were immigrants and my dad comes from a low-income background. My parents have always and still to this day preached that it doesn't matter where you come from; we're all cut from the same cloth. When I was in elementary school, my parents sent me to a school downtown called Coleridge Taylor Elementary. It was located right in the center of one of the toughest places to live in downtown Louisville, where Twany grew up. Majority of the classrooms were 50% black and 50% white.

There were never any questions floating around the school about where people came from. It was a school of kids just being kids. There were only a few occurrences where a kid would act out violently. I can remember one time a kid was cussing out the teacher and being so aggressively disruptive that his mom had to come into the classroom and snatch him up to take him out of there. I had never witnessed things like that before. In those type of scenarios, I would use my observation to experience the situation, but not let that change my friendships, attitudes, or respect towards anyone in the school.

When I made the high school basketball team and became teammates with Twany, that was a success for me. I didn't expect to make it. I didn't grow up playing basketball. I found my desire to play late, around middle school. The kids on the basketball team who came from downtown were our most talented players. They were so much better, quicker and more athletic than me. To me, it was all about how can I prove myself to these guys, hone their trust, and then build the best team around...on and off the court. There wasn't a moment outside of the season that we weren't eating together, watching movies, listening to music or traveling together. It was constant. It took three really strong years to fully build that rapport.

I understood that I was playing alongside a bunch of guys that had already been tested because of where they came from. For me, the most stressful moments of my day were stepping on the basketball court. I knew that I had a limited amount of ability that I had to maximize.

I faced pressures of having to make the open shots because if I didn't, I might not get the ball again. I had to be perfect defensively and be willing to dive on the floor for loose balls. I had to do any and everything to stay on the court with the guys. But, after our two-hour practices ended, I knew that I was going to have a ride home. I knew that I was going to have food on the table. Those things I didn't have to worry about like some of my teammates did.

Some of my teammates started coming home with me to spend the nights and have dinner with my family. My parents loved to help out because they could relate to the situations some of my friends were in, especially my dad. My parents also had that parental foresight of looking at the situation and thinking that these kids can teach our son about things that he will never go through. It was one of the biggest blessings that I could ever ask for. I heard my role model say this the other day, "Life's greatest teacher is experience. You have to go through something or go through something with somebody that's been through it to really gain the rapport from them."

Twany and I are like best friends. There isn't a day that goes by that we don't text or talk on the phone. It's always open communication, always honesty, and always real. We're always pushing each other when need to be pushed. We tell each other to slow down when we need to slow down. It's the same chemistry that we had on the court except we're playing a different game now.

Life is all about adversity. When I think about basketball, I always think about the losses because those were the games from which we learned the most. As a shooter, if you're making shots, that's easy. That's the fun part. But, when those shots aren't going in, are you still going to play defense? Are you still going to communicate with your teammates?

Our coaches used to tell us in high school that if you stop doing those things because you miss a few shots then what are you going to do when you're behind on your bills or your moms needs help? How are you going to overcome real pressures outside of sports? When adversity comes, take a breath, get through it, and then learn from it. That will make you stronger the next time.

To get to anywhere in life you want to go, you're going to have to gut it out when it's tough. I think that's the reason that you do see successful college athletes outside of their sports whether in business or whatever because they already have that work ethic. Hard work and discipline is built into their character and to me, character is

Pressure

something that can't be passed down or taught. It's something that you have to look in the mirror and say I'm going to do this because this is my why and nothing is going to stop me.

I am Chris Gowers and I have survived PRESSURE.

Chapter 2

When I look my biological father in the eyes, I see hurt... I see pain... I see guilt... I see forgiveness...I see happiness... but most importantly, I see myself. I see a man who so desperately wished he could erase the slate and start over. However, I see a man that is now walking in his truths and finding purpose.

Any chance I get to spend time with my father; I force him to rationalize his reasoning for abandoning me as a child. It's not that I don't understand every word that he utters...I just love how raw and open he is about the situation and I use it as a time to learn. Through all of my father's stories, I know what not to do as a father, but I also know what to do as a father.

Being that I am a mature adult who understands how tough life can be at times, my father's stories are never gut wrenching. I empathize with him and give my support because I know how it feels to have no one you can turn to when in desperate need to vent.

I see hundreds of kids whether through television shows or personal stories that I have encountered, resenting their parents or a parent due to abandonment. I wanted to be different. I didn't want that cloud always hovering over me. I figured that if I

Pressure

were ever able to forgive my father and give him a second chance that I could help others who struggle to find comfort in their situation.

I was born in November of 1988. My father also had two daughters who were born in 1988. He was a heavy user of drugs, which he justified as an escape route from life.

when I listen to my father reflect deeply on his life, I get so immersed in his stories that I actually feel like I walked in his shoes. I can feel his pain as he reminisces on the days of his struggles. Giving my father the opportunity to vent to me soothes my soul. No one deserves to hoard that type of pain. His perspective on life and the pressure he was facing having three kids born in the same year was eye opening.

My father always tells me that when I was maybe four or five years old, there were several instances where we had the potential of connecting. Distantly scoping, my father tells me that he would always see me running around the projects with a basketball in my hands. He said he could tell that I was going to be special and it used to hurt him inside seeing me and not having the courage to speak. The fact that he admits being in arm's length of me on several occasions when I was a child and never taking initiatives to speak does hurt, but I also understand why he chose to stay mute.

Why have your precious little boy around you when drugs still controlled your life? There is no telling what I could have been exposed to had he been in my life and continued to use drugs.

When I say that I see myself in my father, I really do. We're almost identical twins and my talents were directly reflective of his. I heard so many stories about my father's days on the basketball court when I was growing up. I've had people that I didn't know approach me and say things like "you play just like your daddy," or "your daddy is a slam dunking legend in our city." I used to look at those people highly confused. I wondered how they knew who my father was and if they knew that I had never met him.

Our personalities are dead on. He can win you over with his charming smile and has a heart full of gold. My father has been drug and alcohol free for 10 plus years. He gives back to his community by sharing his story and providing moral support to recovering addicts.

Pressure

He is a self-prescribed chef and has two little kids that he can't live without. I love it for my little brother and sister because my dad is getting to write his wrongs with them. They are getting the best version of Eric Dean Tooley.

What if I had resented and held a grudge towards my father for the rest of my life...we both would have never had the opportunity to heal our wounds. Holistically, there would have always been a void within the both of us. There would be no way he could love my little brother and sister the way that he does because his non-relationship with me would still linger in the back of his mind.

The moral of what I am trying to say is, learn to forgive. Having the ability to forgive my father for not being there has helped both of us in ways that are unexplainable.

The only real pressure in this whole situation was my uncertainty of how my mother would react to our relationship. Luckily, my mother never saw a problem with me wanting to get to know my father. Actually, she encouraged it. She has never held any grudges towards my father or has made him pay a penny of child support. For those reasons, my father respects her gracefully.

How many grudges are you holding in your life? Who is that family member or close friend that you haven't spoken to or forgiven? We often times don't realize it, but having ill feelings towards others or refusing to forgive is counterproductive for our psyche.

I challenge you to put an end to all grudges. We only have one life to live. Let's not leave this earth with any regrets.

Pressure made me who I am

Eric Dean Tooley

When my son was born, it was the best day of my life but I was not ready to be a father. I was 24 years old, but I was still a little boy in terms of how I thought and made decisions. I also had two other daughters that were born in the same year. I wanted to be a father and be there for my kids but the responsibilities were frightening. I was scared and typically when people get scared, they have certain mechanisms of how they deal with the situation. The thing that I did was run because that is what I had always done when I faced life situations. Usually when people run away from their problems, they have a false sense of hope that those problems will automatically work themselves out, but life does not work that way. There are still times today where I struggle with facing the reality of some situations and I would rather run and let it play out.

Thirty years ago, when Twany was born, it was not the norm for men living in the projects to fully be there for their kids. It was a regular thing to see single women raising kids by themselves. My father was never consistently around so I never experienced what a father was supposed to be like unless I saw it on the television. I was too bull-headed to ask for help when I know I should have.

When my kids were born, I bounced around in the restaurant industry and made a little money here and there. I always thought that I did not have enough money to help the mothers of my kids out financially. In reality, I was always spending the money that I did have on personal enjoyment. I had no clue of financial responsibility. Once again, I was never shown. With having three kids and already believing that I did not have enough money to help out, my mentality was "screw it". I cannot help anyway. There was no possibility that I was going to contribute. This used to leave me hopeless. There is not any other way to put this. I was selfish.

My mindset around the time Twany was born was... daddy is daddy and mama is mama. Debra and I lived in the same neighborhood so we had experienced many of the same things. The good thing about all of this was, Debra and I were best friends and we knew that everything was going to be okay. Debra was a strong woman. I knew she would take very well care of her kids. I always knew that once I got my life together and got on the right track, that I could genuinely be in my son's life. In life, you only get one mother and one father. I could not let this opportunity to slip away forever.

Even though I wasn't always around my son, I kept a close eye on him from afar. I would call my friends who were close to him and his mother and check to see how he was doing. As Twany and I got to know one another, I still allowed him space to see if he wanted me to fully be a part of his life. The best thing that I could do for myself and for my kids was get myself together and then let them determine if I was somebody who they wanted to deal with.

Once I got myself together, I knew I was ready to step into that role that I should have a long time ago. I say my blessings all the time for my kids allowing me to be in their lives. I also had to accept the fact that it very well could've never happened. I knew of fathers who never got the chance to rekindle with their children, so I was always afraid that it could happen to me.

The lesson that I have taken from all of this is that, the things that happen to you along your journey are vital to who you become. I like who I am now. I do not like the path that I had to take to get here, but what happened to me has help mold me into who I am as a parent to all of my kids. I have eight kids and I am consistently in all of their lives. You have to learn from your mistakes. Life is one day at a time and there is no perfect script. I have learned that a person must have their own life together before they can do anything for anyone else. When you get yourself together first, things around you seem to work out a little better. If you are not together, you can hurt the people you love. You can drag your loved ones down and not even realize that your dragging them down. This is very important for a man to do before he makes the decision that he is ready to be a father.

I am Eric Dean and I have survived PRESSURE.

Chapter 3

Think about the concept of pressure and how pressure applies within the trajectory of your life. It can appear in so many different forms and variations, some of which can be seen or felt. Pressure can mean so many different things depending on who you ask.

How I define pressure can be very different than how you define pressure. How I respond to pressure can be very different than how you respond to pressure.

The goal is for you and I to immerse ourselves in our own pressures and never become negatively impacted. We should become equipped mentally and physically to overcome anything life throws at us.

That's the beauty within life itself. Each individual is different. I can most certainly assure you that every individual in this entire world has gone through some type of pressure that no one else can relate to.

Think about the kids who grow up in poverty-stricken areas without a father, just like me, or the kid that is born and immediately put up for adoption. Think about the girl who gets pregnant at a young age and contemplates abortion. Think about the kids that are raised in a household with two successful parents,

Pressure

but struggle with real life situations because of being spoon fed for so many years. Think about the family whose child is born with downs syndrome or any other disability. That's just the tip of the iceberg, I could ramble on for hours.

When I think about pressure, I feel gratified...only because I understand how challenging life's pressures can be and what type of person my pressures have turned me into. I feel like I have risen from underneath a rock that has been stepped on a million times...a rock that set out to specifically crush and kill anything that it met.

I've heard for so many years that getting out of the projects and going to college was going to be one of the best feelings in the entire world. When you think about it, how could it not...especially going to college to play basketball? Not many people from my family ever went to college and not many from the neighborhood did either so it was definitely something at the top of my list of goals.

When God blessed me with the tremendous opportunity to attend college on an athletic scholarship eight hours away in Mississippi, I thought that I had achieved the inevitable. I felt like I tore down barriers. I viewed myself as someone who had essentially made it. However, I still had holes in my happiness. I struggled with feeling like I left my family behind.

Phone calls and texts about the pleasurable time I was having probably did more damage than I realized. All I wanted was for somebody to be happy for me.

My younger brother, who played alongside me in sports since we were young kids, didn't get the opportunity to play sports in college. He was a great football player, but the cards didn't fall in his favor to extend his career after high school. I believed, stumbling upon the perfect opportunities, he could've had a chance at the NFL.

I remember the last basketball game we played together and I will never forget the words he uttered to me in the locker room after the game. We had lost a heart breaker in the championship game of the state tournament. To this day, the thought of that game, leaves a sour taste in my mouth.

Plumped over in a cubby inside the locker room with a towel over my head drenched in tears, my brother hugged me and joined in. Barely being able to utter his words, he said,

Pressure

"I'm going to miss playing with you and you will always be my big brother for life."

I grabbed him and said, "I got you forever and you come back and win this thing next year."

That was the last thing he was trying to hear come out of my mouth. Reality was setting in that we will never be teammates again...ever in life. Even though we are only eleven months apart, my little brother deemed me as his role model.

As I'm off and experiencing the perks of being a NCAA Division One athlete at a power five conference school, I felt removed from the pressures that plagued me throughout the first eighteen years of my life. I felt like I had escaped the pressures that come with living in the projects... gangs, fights, bullets, etc. I felt like I had escaped the stresses that plagued our family...bills, family issues etc. I felt like I owed it to myself to centralize Twany as the focal point of my life and not worry about anything other than myself.

Who was I fooling? I probably worried more being eight hours away than I did being at home.

Twany Beckham

I always thought about what was going on back at home and how my family was doing. I thought about my friends who were still trapped in the cycles of poverty and often times wondered if they'd ever be fortunate to make it out.

My childhood best friend was murdered while I was away at school. I can remember my family calling me to share the news.

My soul was demolished. That could've been me.

A couple of weeks prior to his death, he sent me a message on Facebook telling me how proud he was of me and that he couldn't wait to come and visit me at school. I received plenty more of those shocking calls about different friends that I grew up with while I was away at college.

The two and a half years that I was eight hours away, my family came to visit me once, but that one time was amazingly special. My brother and several of my cousins all came and we had a blast. I was so excited to show my family how I was living on a big-time college campus…my brother especially.
My family couldn't have chosen a better weekend to come to visit me. We had a major Television game on the schedule. We were matched up against

Pressure

Tennessee, who were one of the best teams in the South-Eastern Conference (SEC) that year.
I remember running out of the tunnel to a packed Humphrey Coliseum and seeing my family standing up cheering with the rest of the crowd... You talk about chills...emotional roller-coaster.

For the first time, I felt true happiness!!!

I felt the ramifications of putting a smile on someone else's face. I felt what it was like to provide an opportunity of a lifetime to someone. I felt the impact and experienced the true meaning of using your gifts and successes to bring joy to others.

After the game, my brother and I shared a hug, but to hear his full commentary about the game felt amazing. I could tell he didn't take his eyes off of the court for a single second.

Fast forward a few years, I've graduated from college...my brother and I are roommates...and we were both trying to figure out life.

I was doing my own thing and he was doing his own thing. We loved living together because we got to catch up on so much lost time. I think my mother loved it more than we did because she knew that I would help my brother evolve in areas in which I was proficient.

One day, those feelings that I struggled with as a freshman in college, came between a tiny gap of air between me and my brother's noses. We were standing face to face in our condo screaming at each other over a disagreement and every negative emotion imaginable flooded the room. My brother said a few things to me that I had always felt in my head and that day he clarified it.

He said some things to me that really made me feel guilty about everything I had ever worked for. Even though I told him how pathetic his views were at the time, he actually made points that made sense. Out of all the things that he said, these are the words that I saw come out of his mouth in slow motion that I will never forget….

> "You left us when you went to college. You don't know what it's like to struggle."

It was laborious listening to my brother say those things to me. I felt like he forgot the fact that we actually lived in the same house for eighteen years and shared many of the same experiences. However, in another breath, I understood the hole in which he was pulling from. He had experienced a couple tough years and the adversity he faced was unfathomable to me.

It was healthy to relieve that pressure and animosity that held weight between us. I never actually thought he and I would ever have that type of conversation. He brought out the guilt that I wrestled with on many restless nights, but I understood exactly where he was coming from. I escaped the pressure for several years while he had to marinate in it and watch me live a fun life. That's a tough pill to swallow, especially when we've been tied at the hip for our entire lives... a wall separating our bedrooms.

Pressure made me who I am

Andre Gardner Jr.

My brother Twany and I had a great relationship growing up. The identity of our relationship really developed throughout elementary and middle school when we both started playing basketball and football together. I was just a grade under Twany, so I always got to play at least one year with him...whether it was football or basketball. I always looked up to him not only as a big brother but as a mentor as well.

When we got into high school, I really started to pay attention to how everything was shaping up for Twany. We both started to go our own ways. Football was my thing and basketball was his thing. I played on the high school basketball team just so I could be his teammate. I didn't progress like I thought I should but my brother's career just took off. I watched his notoriety around the city shoot through the roof. He had all of the city fame. More and more people started flocking to my brother than they did me and that use to really bother me. What bothered me the most was that the majority of the people who payed me no attention and gave it all to Twany, were a lot of our family members. I felt like I was always pushed to the side. Everyone saw Twany as the next ticket out of here.

The last game that my brother and I were teammates was probably the greatest atmosphere I'd ever been in. There are some things you just don't get the luxury of experiencing twice so that game was very important to me. It wasn't certain that if we lost that I was going to be back in the state title game as a senior. The game before the championship game, I hit my head and had to go into concussion protocol but I was determined to play that last game with my brother. We were also facing the only team that had beaten us in the state of Kentucky that year, so I wanted the payback in the big game. It was my brothers last high school game ever. I knew how bad he wanted it. I will never forget after the loss how personal I took it. People kept coming up to me in the locker room telling me that I had next year and like I've mentioned, next year isn't promised. You have to live for today. After that game, my brother told me that he always had my back no matter what as he was moving on with his journey.

When Twany went off to college, it was tough. I was still trying to figure out which path in life I was going to take. I was really happy for my brother. He was chasing his dreams. With him being gone, I felt like I had no one there to support me outside of my mother. My brother was always one phone call away but it wasn't the same as physically having him around.

I struggled with trying to find decent jobs to take care of myself. When you come from where we come from, you're taught to chase sports or get involved in the streets in order to make it out. I can honestly say that I never took school as serious as I could have because I was so focused on using sports to make it out. I never had the opportunity to work a job until I got out of high school. Everything with me had to deal with sports. I was clueless about the real world. Things that I learned in school paid me no dividend in the real world.

When my brother returned home from college and we were living together, we bumped heads on several occasions. I feel like there were a lot of things that he didn't understand from being away for so long. We clashed over things that I didn't think Twany was ever going to grasp until he started living a regular life like I was. To me, college is not hard if you dedicate yourself in the classroom and do what you have to do on the court. That should be easy. If you miss a class or let's say a tutoring session or something, worst case scenario, you may miss a game or face some small disciplinary actions. In the real world, if you miss work or show up late, you can be fired on the spot. If you have rent to pay and you don't pay it, the consequences result in you getting kicked out of your apartment. Those are just some pressures that I faced while my brother was away at college.

My brother mentioned all the time that he stressed and couldn't fully enjoy college because of being worried about us back at home. We didn't intentionally want to have that burden on him. We wanted him to stay as focused as possible because he was doing something that could potentially benefit the family. We tried to keep as many issues out of his sight as we could. As for me and mom, we were living every single day in the struggle.

I have overcome all the pressures in life because I have failed so many times. I believe in order to be successful you have to learn how to bounce back from failure. I've had temp job after temp job after temp job and things for a while just didn't go my way.

One time, I had a good job and then my car messed up and I couldn't get to work. Things happen, but you have to figure out a way to overcome them. When my father passed away, I think that catapulted my ambition and my drive to want more out of life. Where we are from, you're dead by 18 or in jail by 25 and to make it past that is a blessing. We have friends and family that are dead and for me and my brother to make it out and be living healthy lives is a blessing. He has seen me evolve. I have seen him evolve. My daughter has helped me change as a man, as well. Twany really changed and became a man after having his dreams stripped away from him. My brother and I are closer than ever and nothing will ever break that bond.

    I am Andre Gardner Jr and I have survived **PRESSURE.**

One of the strongest relationships I have with someone outside of family and friends is with a man that I befriended while in high school named Stan Whitaker. Our relationship hasn't always been easy to figure out and the pressure of maintaining our relationship over the years, at times, has been rough. I befriended Mr. Whitaker while trying to prepare to take the ACT test. He and his wife, both retired educators, helped young men like myself prepare for that daunting test.

Our relationship got off to a rocky start. I missed several scheduled tutoring appointments and almost severed ties with someone who was trying to help me. I tried to make excuses to justify why I missed the appointments because my mind was still flustered with questions.

Who was Mr. Whitaker?
Why was he choosing to help me?
What was he looking to get out of it?
What were his motives?

I remember seeing Mr. Whitaker after one of my basketball games and he joked with me about me dissing his tutoring sessions. After the third or fourth attempt, I finally made a session and he and I have never looked back. We just clicked. He had this funny personality that I fell in love with. I started calling him every day just to check in with him and he did the same. He had this way about him that just allowed me to be open and free around him. I trusted him. Any free time that I had, I would go to his home and he and I would sit and talk about life for hours. I've told him things that only he, God and I know about. He has consulted with me about all of my problems and has always managed to guide me through them.

I've learned so many life skills from being around Mr. Whitaker. My dinner etiquette skills are profound enough that I can teach them to you. I've learned how to treat others with complete respectfulness. I've learned how to be sociable in a manner in which I'm confident but yet humbled. The list can go on.......

You may think that the lessons I mentioned were simple but if you're never educated on certain things in life, how would you ever expect to know certain things.

Mr. Whitaker and I would go to dinner and before our meal arrived, he made me go up to random people in the restaurant and introduce myself. This drove me nuts, but I had to do it. That really got me out of my shell. The funny thing about going to dinner with Mr. Whitaker was people would come over to our table and ask what the relation was between the two of us. Mr. Whitaker would always refer to me as his son and you would have thought that people saw a ghost. He said it so often that I just started calling him "Pops."

Still to this day, people look at us funny when we're out together. I've had family and friends question the relationship. I've had people question whether or not I was using him for his money. I've had someone tell me not to refer to a white man as my "Pops". I have heard it all. I guess because he was white and I was black, it was hard for people to accept.

My mother never once questioned the relationship and was very thankful that someone took the time to extend a helping hand.

Being around Mr. Whitaker helped shape my profound love of being a mentor to kids. He is a mentor to me so I feel as if I am obligated to give back and pay it forward.

Mr. Whitaker often challenges my thought process on the manners in which I love to live my life. He grew up very different from me so his outlook on life was shaped significantly different. He has challenged a lot of my materialistic ways and has put me in situations to allow me to see the bigger picture.

I can remember a conversation that he and I had that I will never forget. I was back in town from Atlanta visiting because I hadn't been home in a while. It was obvious that I had to stop by "Pops" house to see him. In the midst of shooting the breeze, he asked me how life was treating me in Atlanta and if I was satisfied with my job. I immediately started venting about how I should be making more money, doing this, and doing that. He stopped me in my tracks and said,

> "Until you go and work at McDonalds, you will never be humbled. You will never know what it feels like to start from the bottom."

The room silenced.

He and I stared at each for two minutes while tears slowly ran down my face. "You're right Pops," I said very calmly.

Even though I was somewhat confused by his comment of me never knowing what it felt like to start from the bottom, I emotionally didn't have the energy to question his logic. I wondered if he had forgotten about where I came from but I didn't want to miss his point so I kept quiet.

Whenever Pops and I reminisce and talk about how much I've progressed throughout the years, we always refer back to that conversation. Even though I have never worked at McDonalds, I definitely understood the humility he was trying to instill in me. I am willing to bet that ever since that day, no one, and I mean no one, has worked harder than I have.

Pressure made me who I am

Stan Whitaker

I was raised the last of 12 children. I experienced not having a lot of things that maybe I wished I could've had. I had other people who helped me in life besides my family. Although, I had help from my family, there were other caring people who seemed to always be there for me and I wanted to pay that forward. I saw that if it can make that much difference in me, then I can make that much difference in someone else. My whole life, I have always felt that every day, you should try to make a difference in someone's life.

Pressure

I was a principal for 20 years and a college professor for 10 years and my wife, Bonny, is a retired teacher. When we both retired, we decided to start helping kids prepare for the ACT test. Early on in my life, I enjoyed attending athletic events in the small town where I grew up. Athletic events were one of the few social events that we had. After retiring, my wife and I still enjoyed attending athletic events and I started asking people "what happened to that young man or young lady?" and people would always tell me that he or she couldn't get into college because they couldn't pass the ACT test. I wondered how athletes could stay eligible every week, play in every game and then disappear when their athletic eligibility was over. At that point, my wife and I said to each other, "Let's try to make a difference". We knew that you couldn't teach kids all of the subject matter, but you could help kids learn how to take tests. The ACT or the SAT tests are developed by people who are looking for standards. They base those upon standards of what they think a graduating senior from a school in the United States should have. We just did not believe that the kids here in the state of Kentucky were that much in deficit compared to kids all over the United States. But, we saw that kids from Kentucky always scored lower compared to kids in most other states. We did this from about 1994 until 2017. We have helped over 500 kids. We had several students participate once or twice and never came back.

One of the pressures with helping people and especially kids, in the manner that we did, was that we always had to be battle resistant. In order for kids to receive help, they have to be present. They have to show up. One of our biggest issues was, getting kids interested in coming to scheduled tutoring for the testing. Especially, when I'm being told already that the kids aren't motivated. Society, the schools and the test scores, tell us that you can't make a difference on a kid's test scores. But, we felt like we could. Did all of the kids improve...NO, but the ones who were serious and wanted to improve... did. Were there kids that we wanted to improve that didn't improve...YES. I can remember being out of town one evening and getting a call from a kid with pure excitement about scoring a 21 on his ACT test which was the best score he had ever gotten. Getting those types of calls is what made everything worth it.

I remember seeing Twany Beckham when he was in middle school, play in a middle school basketball tournament. I thought to myself, this kid is a pretty good basketball player...never thinking that we would ever work with him to help him improve his test scores. Maybe two years later, we were at another basketball tournament that Twany was playing in and I said to someone who knew him, "He'll probably have a very good college career". This person said to me, "I don't think so because I don't think he has the academics to go to college." I said, well that's really a shame that he doesn't have the academics and I asked this person why they thought that and they mentioned Twany's low scores on the ACT prep test. Now of course, in my mind, when someone tells me someone can't do something, I think the opposite. I thought to myself; let's give this kid a chance. I just so happened to be at the home of another student that I was helping and Twany was leaving the home. When I saw him, I said, "Aren't you Twany Beckham" and he said, "Yes." I said "Well, my wife and I do ACT prep and I would like for you to come." He said, "Well, maybe." And, we never saw him. Now, his friends came and I used to ask them, "Where is Twany?" They would always say Twany will never come. I saw Twany again and asked him about coming and he didn't show up again. I then got the feeling that it wasn't me but the fear he had of taking the test and proving what he believed other people thought. I thought Twany didn't want to run the risk of letting anyone know that he didn't have the ability to pass the test. Twany completely shut out the thought of taking of the test and I wasn't sure if he ever took the test or not.

I discussed this situation with someone very close to Twany because I was really worried about what he would do after high school. He was a great athlete and a great kid. I was worried about what was going to happen next. I didn't want to see him waste it. When Twany made the decision that he was going to attend a prep school, I was happy for him. We talked every day and it was kind of like a tutoring session over the phone. I always checked with him about how school was going and he would share every single thing that he was learning. We would talk a lot about what he was reading and some of the things he was studying. I took a trip up to New Hampshire to visit Twany at his prep school to meet the teachers and to see how he was doing.

I would describe our relationship currently as a friendly, advisory, sometimes I told you so, better think about this, type of relationship. Although, I say to him a lot of times that I should tell you the exact opposite of what to do because he's really never done anything I've ever asked him to do. We both get a good laugh out to that.

To overcome the pressures in life, one needs to develop self-worth. You have to realize that it's not about the person whose helping, it's about the person whose being helped. Often, people want to help people but they want something for it. I have always been taught that if you do something good for someone and you tell someone about it, then it wasn't a good deed. If you do something good for someone and you run and tell everyone about it, then what were your motives? Why did you want to do something for someone if you were going to immediately go talk about it? I will always stand by this – if you really want to do something for someone, you don't have to take any credit for it. If I can help someone develop self-worth, then it helps change their environment, their culture, their desire to succeed in life and also helps fuel their desires to help someone else.

I am Stan Whitaker and I have survived PRESSURE.

Chapter 4

When I was 7 years old, I made a promise to myself that I was going to make it to the NBA and help get my family out of poverty. Yes, that sounded good and was probably the same thing every other young athlete promised themselves that also lived in impoverished communities around the world.

What I didn't understand was the amount of pressure that I was putting on myself. I now had a whole family that I put on my back and was willing to use the talents God blessed me with to make a way for them. I approached life every day with the mentality of NBA or nothing. This gave my life great purpose, which also added great pressure. I no longer lived with a free and clear mind.

I now had to take in account of the thoughts and feelings of my family before I made any decisions. I couldn't allow for one bad decision on my behalf to impact my family in any negative capacity. Basketball games weren't just basketball games anymore. Each game was a game closer to getting my family and I to the NBA and out of poverty.

After I graduated from high school, my future was uncertain. Before my senior season started, I signed a

Pressure

letter of intent to play basketball at Indiana University Purdue University of Indianapolis (IUPUI) but I de-committed midway through my senior year. I committed to IUPUI early in my recruitment process because their coaches recruited me the hardest and I felt that the interest was genuine from both sides. I also got tired of all the pressure that college coaches were putting on me. All the calls, persuasive letters and meetings got tiresome and I wanted it to be over. I also wanted to select a college before my senior season started so that I could focus on winning a state title.

I ended up having a season that was better than I expected and everyone around me that I trusted thought I should reconsider my college choice and attend a prep school for more exposure. I reached out, received calls from prep schools, and landed an opportunity to visit a school located in New Hampshire called the New Hampton School.

My visit went really well. I loved the coach and everything the school offered athletically and academically. The school had produced numerous high major division one players and I was looking forward to becoming next in line. On the final day of my visit, as all the visiting incoming players were getting set to head to the airport to return home until school started, my coach hit me with some news that I wasn't expecting…. pressure.

Coach told me that I was going to be his starting point guard but in order for me to be able to enroll in classes, I had to come up with a $1,700 entry fee. Before he could even get the last digits out of his mouth, I almost told him "thank you for the opportunity but no way do I have the means for meeting that obligation."

My family didn't have that type of money and I didn't have a clue of who or where I could even ask for help. But, before I could even utter a single word, coach already had a solution. He told me that I wasn't going back home to Kentucky for the rest of the summer and that I was going to stay in New Hampshire and work around the community to raise the money. If my initial thoughts would have come out of my mouth, I probably wouldn't be where I am today.

I had never lived away from my mom and brothers and to have this randomly thrown at me, wasn't something I had envisioned getting out of this visit. There was one other player that stayed back with me because he too had to come up with the entry fee.

Pressure

Would you have agreed to stay in New Hampshire to work and miss your entire summer right after graduating from high school? Would you have trusted a coach that you barely knew and believed that he had your best interest in mind? How many of you would have just searched for another prep school to attend that didn't have such a steep entry fee? At eighteen years old, making these decisions on my own was pressure. As much as I would've loved to take the easy route and search for another prep school, I decided to stay and work primarily because something in me trusted this coach. Something in me saw the bigger picture.

Every morning, Monday through Friday, Coach Hutchins would pick us up at the front door of the dorm around 8:00 a.m. and drive us to our work station for the day. We took on the responsibility of cleaning lake houses, boats, garages, mopping floors, and also raking leaves in extremely large yards…. work that I had never done before.

After finishing with work for the day, we would eat dinner and then head to the gym for a workout to end our day. I improved so much as a basketball player during this time and so did my work ethic. This was the first time ever that I had access to a gym fifty yards from where I lived. I wanted to sleep in there some nights.

We definitely had our times where I thought Coach Hutchins was going to send us home. One morning when Coach came to pick us up, neither my teammate or I felt like going so we didn't answer our phones. When coach came in the dorm to get us, we both hid and staged our room to make it look like we had already left. We heard Coach storm out of the dorm very frustrated. There were several of those occurrences throughout that summer but coach never gave up on us. We were able to raise the money to pay our entry fee!!!

That one year of prep school worked out perfectly for me. I attracted interest from major colleges and I improved drastically as a student. I had never come close to being ranked nationally, but after my one year of prep school, I was ranked in the top 15 of all prep school players in the country. I earned a scholarship to play division one basketball at Mississippi State University.

My family and I were just one stop short of our destination.

Pressure

You would think once I got to college that life would be sweet because that's what I always strived for. It was the complete opposite. Life hit me and the pressure got so big I almost couldn't handle it.

Several weeks before my first official college game and in the midst of one of the toughest competition battles I had ever faced, I fractured a bone in my foot and missed the start of my freshman basketball season. Before my injury, I was neck and neck with the other freshman point guard fighting to see who would get the nod on opening night.

The summer after my freshman season, I was diagnosed with having bone spurs on both of my hips and had to undergo surgery to have them removed. I sat out my entire sophomore season and limped to class on crutches the entire year. It took everything in me mentally and physically not to break down and give up. Double hip surgery was the most painful thing I had ever experienced.

In my mind, my NBA dreams took a bit of a hit. What NBA team would want a player with bad hips? I couldn't settle with letting my mind think that way. I tried to trick my mind into thinking of how sweet it would be to have overcome those hurdles and still make it.

Twany Beckham

As I was preparing for my senior season and my last legitimate shot at making a career out of basketball, I woke up one morning and felt my dreams leave my body. I rolled out of bed and had no feeling in my legs. I knew at that moment that my life was about to take a turn for the worst.

I was soon after diagnosed with having two herniated discs in my back...L4-L5. My doctor suggested surgery being the best route to take long term but I needed instant gratification. I needed feeling back in my legs so that I could play in my senior season. I received three epidurals but the relief each time was only temporary.

It wasn't the devastating news that broke me, or having no feeling in my legs that had me worried. It was the fact that I wouldn't be able to deliver on the promise that I made when I was seven years old. My cries lasted for years.........

I doubt that my family ever understood the amount of pressure that I placed on myself from the time I was seven years old. I doubt that my mother and two younger brothers ever realized that I was willing to die to see them live stress free. Basketball was my first love and will always be but I took the fun out of it when I made that promise to myself. Everything

Pressure

became very business structured and I stopped enjoying the game.

I can remember a point in my career when I was living my dream playing for the University of Kentucky and I was miserable. I wasn't getting much playing time. No one understood the pressure I had within myself to make it and every game that I didn't get to play sabotaged my stock.

The pressure to make it got to me so much that I started to hate basketball. I sat on the bench and watched others raise their stock night in and night out. It was so tough to cheer on my teammates but when it got that bad, I knew that something was wrong. Struggling with finding happiness for someone you go to war with every day is a problem I had to fix within myself. After games, I would run to my family and friends to complain but that obviously wasn't going to fix anything.

I will never forget coming out of the locker room after a home game early in my junior season. My mother, brothers and my cousin Kevin were in attendance. It was the very first game that I was eligible to play at Kentucky. I was a transfer so I had to sit out an entire season before I could compete in a game. I was so pumped to finally have the opportunity of checking into a basketball game with KENTUCKY written across my chest.

THIS WAS MY DREAM!!!!!

We were playing the University of Chattanooga, a school that had offered me a scholarship while I was in high school. I was really excited to play against them. The media attention surrounding me the week leading up to the game was insane. Every reporter wanted to gather my thoughts to gage my feelings of finally being eligible to play.

My entire family was tuned into their TV's to witness what I would call history for my family. As the game was going on and going on, I kept staring up at the clock to see minute after minute ticking away. I kept looking down the bench hopeful that coach would look my way or call my name to check in. Nothing.

We were up by a ton of points with very little time left on the game clock when I finally heard my name called. By that time, eighty five percent of Rupp arena had already bolted for the exits and I had lost my enthusiasm for wanting any parts of the game. I checked in with the worst attitude imaginable and my body language was a direct representation. I jogged up and down the court with lack luster effort during those final possessions and felt very embarrassed.

After the game, I pouted like a baby. My mother and cousin ripped into me fiercely. They definitely helped me and everyone else in the locker room area who tuned in understand how I was taking my opportunities for granted. They repeatedly drove home the fact that I was living a dream and doing something only a very few get to do. My mother demanded that my attitude change. I didn't say a word. I just looked at my brother, mom and cousin with teary eyes, wanting so badly to yell at them,

> *"I want this so bad for you all and not playing won't help with that."*

That still may not have helped. No one understood the pressure that I had in my head but me.

From that moment on, I changed as an individual, a son and a teammate. Once again, I was humbled. I started to appreciate things a little more and took less for granted. My family was right. I was living my dreams playing for the University of Kentucky and how I was taking that for granted started to baffle me.

I became the best teammate my teammates could have asked for. Practice became my games. I brought it every single day of practice to make myself and my teammates better. My attitude went from one of the worst on the team to one of the best on the team.

I was truly finding happiness within myself just by changing my attitude and appreciating my opportunities.

Sometimes it would hit me that my NBA chances were dwindling, but at that point, I was happy and fulfilled.

You ever wondered why we go through adversity or why certain things happen to you that you don't understand? Life to me, is almost like playing a game; two steps forward and then one step back. It takes an incredible amount of sacrifice to get to the finish line. It took a while for me to actually understand that everything happens for a reason and when looking back on my life, I'm actually thankful for the process that brought me to where I am today!

I have now figured out my purpose in life. But, did basketball have to be taken away from me in order for me to start living my purpose? Had I not had back surgery, I wonder if I would still be chasing a professional basketball career and doing so for all the reasons in the world except for me. Would I have self-published one book already if I were still playing basketball? Would I be in communities inspiring kids to chase their dreams and giving the perspective of one who has? Would I be traveling the world inspiring people to change their culture? Are you starting to get the picture? Even though, these questions will theoretically never be answered, I pretty much feel like all the adversity that I have endured prepared me for the life that I currently live.

Some of us discover our passion later in life but you should always be thankful for your struggles along the way. I proudly say that because as you've read so far, I am not doing what I envisioned doing when I was growing up. My life took a few bumps, bruises, turns and sleepless nights before I actually found something that I was passionate about.

There are people in life that run from their struggles or hate themselves because of the things that have occurred in their lives. I am here to tell you, LOVE YOUR STRUGGLES! Appreciate every negative emotion or feeling that you have felt. We would not be the people we are without them.

Dreams fail, we lose jobs, we run out of money, we lose friends and we lose motivation. I could go on and on about the daily struggles we face. However, what I can tell you is that all of this makes us stronger. The struggles are pressures placed on you to test your inner strengths. The comfortable and easy route to take is to let the pressure get the best of you and quit.

No one respects a quitter.

Now, let's switch over to you for a second. Have you put yourself in similar types of situations that I found myself in? Have you made any promises or added large amounts of pressure to your life? Have you faced tons of adversity? I would venture to say that the majority of you probably nodded your head yes to those questions. If you did, take a second and think about how you've dealt with those pressures in your life and how you've responded to adversity. Did you lose your mind when things didn't go your way?

Give yourself a pat on the back because you've survived such trying times and if you're in the midst of the struggle right now... Just know... I AM PRAYING FOR YOUR STRENGTH.

Pressure made me who I am

Jamal Crook

My mother was the muscle of our family. I never had my father around when I was young. My mother was working all these night jobs to make ends meet. I would always see her coming into the house in the mornings really tired. That's some stuff that you just don't want to see or want your mother going through. Knowing that I had the opportunity through sports to try to help the situation was something that I could not take advantage of. I had to take sports really serious because it was our only way out. I just wanted to be able to make some type of money to help my mother out so that she didn't have to struggle anymore.

I didn't have any role models in sports or anyone to show me the successful ways to go about making it. I had an older brother who graduated from college and he was the biggest influencer in my life, educationally. I had to face the pressures of getting everything on my own. I literally had to teach myself how to play basketball because I didn't have anyone else to teach me. I had to find my own rides to gyms and catch buses home on most nights.

All of the struggles and hard work payed off for me. I earned a scholarship to play basketball at Western Kentucky University. My senior season was the most critical point of my career. I actually thought that I had a shot. I was one year from making it to play professionally. I just needed to have a great year. Several pre-season publications had me listed as a Player of the Year candidate for our conference.

The beginning of the season started off great for me. I was averaging 19.5 points and around 5 assists per game. My situation could not have been set up any better. Ten games into the season, we were playing against Murray State University and Isaiah Canaan who was on every NBA draft board as a first round pick. This was an opportunity to make a name for myself. Five minutes into the game, I fractured my foot.

Doctors told me that I could potentially miss the remainder of my senior season. Besides the struggles I faced growing up, that was probably the toughest times I ever faced in my life. I cried religiously. I really thought I was going to be able to help with my family before my injury. My trainer forced a mindset on me that helped me approach rehab like a beast every day. He told me not to worry about how many games that I was missing but to focus on coming back a beast.

Pressure

After getting healthy and having an opportunity to play basketball professionally oversees, I tore my ACL, which is something all athletes fear. It's very rare for athletes to fully recover from an ACL injury. I not only tore it once, I tore it a consecutive time.

I overcame the pressures of everything I was going through because I had a great support system from my mother, my brothers, my teammates, the coaching staff and most definitely the trainers. One thing I've learned is that when you're going through tough times, you have to stay positive. I spent about three years of fighting myself trying to hold on to the basketball dream but I finally had to let go. I am thankful for everything that I have endured because it's definitely made me who I am today.

I am Jamal Crook and I have survived PRESSURE.

Chapter 5

Have you ever been at the emergency room for a procedure and the doctor comes in before the procedure and walks you through some last-minute instructions before injecting you with anesthesia? Have you ever payed attention to whether or not, the doctor disclosed to you about the slight chance of you losing your life if you undergo the surgery?

The first time I ever heard those words come out of my doctor's mouth, I was strapped to a surgical bed with IV's running through my arms. I was getting ready to have all four of my wisdom teeth pulled. That was my first time ever being put to sleep for a procedure and it scared the hell out of me. Especially, after the doctor explained that my life could potentially end. The chances of that happening were very slim, but I guess I missed that part of the instructions. My mind was strung out on the possibility.

What amazed me, was the pressure the doctor knew he was facing but how calm his demeanor was.

When we think about the people whose employment consists of protecting and saving lives like doctor's, police officers, and firefighters, you have to associate pressure with those people. When I hear stories

Pressure

about people who have gone through things like open-heart surgery, brain surgery or anything of that nature, I immediately think about the doctors who had to perform the surgery and the pressure they faced with having a life in the palms of their hands.

I often think about the surgeries I've endured and always get that feeling of uneasiness. It's those type of feelings that cloud your mind with all the "what if's." What if my doctor had completely messed up my nervous system and paralyzed me trying to repair my back. What if I could never exercise again or function the way I was accustomed to. Those real-life situations could have occurred.

Now, let's examine the pressure a policeman faces on a day to day basis. Police officers are expected to keep our environment safe. Their daily responsibilities evolve around getting criminals off the streets and sometimes, that's easier said than done.

Nowadays, our social media feeds are saturated with confrontations involving police officers whether its shootings or physical altercations. We live in a time now where people are afraid of police officers and fear for their lives when confronted by one.

People who serve and fight for our country also come to mind when I think about people facing huge pressures to protect and save lives. I knew a friend who served in the US army during the times we were at war with Iraq. It's extremely hard for me to fathom the pressure someone waking up every day in Iraq faced during those times.

I think about the people who are in the world of sales; the world of having to eat what you kill to make a living; having to close a sale in order to put food on the table.

Several months after I graduated from the University of Kentucky, I attended a presentation by an insurance company that sold you on the idea of working on a commission based only structure. The reward for working in that type of environment was having unlimited opportunity of making lots of money. If you were hired, you had to complete a couple days of training and then you were off and running...building your book of business.

Joining this agency caught my attention because of the picture the owner of the agency painted. All I saw was the potential of earning lots of money but I didn't think about how much pressure it would be to make a sale. I decided to take a chance and give it a shot.

My first couple of days on the job, I spent a lot of time making cold calls just to be cursed out and hung up on. I headed home late on most nights very frustrated. I pressed on several appointments because I was desperately trying to get the sale. I learned very quickly that when you appear to be desperate, customers can sure sense it.

After a full two weeks of repeating this cycle, I decided that working in a commission based only career wasn't conducive for my life at that time. I didn't have enough in my savings account that would have allowed me to work for practically nothing until I built my book of business.

TOO MUCH PRESSURE.

Think about the pressure our teachers face on a day-to-day basis and how they shoulder the load with being responsible for educating our generations. When parents send their kids off to school, they are expecting their kid to receive excellent and adequate education. When a kid doesn't do well in the classroom, it's primarily the teachers who take the blame.

I was that student that frustrated teachers because I was very intelligent, but I never applied myself. I always got by doing the bare minimum of what was required academically.

I can't count how many times teachers reminded me about having to do well in the classroom in order to play sports at the collegiate level. In my earlier years of grade school, hearing that over and over didn't come across as motivational for me. Some of my friends and I fought the pressure of survival every day in our neighborhoods, so doing school work was sometimes the last thing on our minds.

When I was in the 4th grade, a childhood friend of mine was killed in a drive by shooting while lying down in her house. The news was devastating because that could have easily been anyone of us in the neighborhood.

On occasions, teachers have to deal with kids who come from and witness traumatic situations like I just mentioned and that could be very challenging. One of the best pleasures I get out of life is when I visit schools to interact with the kids and get the opportunity to sit down with the ones who misbehave. Those kids can disrupt an entire class and make a teacher's life miserable.

Pressure

One time I walked into a classroom and witnessed a student punching other students and was inches away from attacking the teacher, had I not been there to intervene. That teacher was one of the nicest people you would ever meet and really harmless. I asked the kid why he was acting in such horrible fashion and he alluded to being mad about something outside of school.

In today's society, where the poverty levels are reaching all-time highs in some parts of the county, the difficulty between teacher/student relationships are enhancing. We have children in our society who have to adult themselves each and every single day. We have children in our society who are on the brink of starvation as they enter classrooms. We have children who are physically harmed and bullied daily.

Put yourself in those child's shoes. Would you be able to focus in the classroom if your main objective is to survive every day? Would you be able to focus in school if you were hungry, bullied or physically harmed by your parents?

I can see where a kid would have limited interest in learning when faced with those pressures. Teachers don't always know what goes on in the lives of these kids before they get to school which makes it difficult from both perspectives. However, I do believe that teachers are huge amplifiers in our society for changing the lives of our children.

Pressure made me who I am

NyRee Clayton-Taylor

I grew up in the Chickasaw Park area that is located downtown in the west end of Louisville, Kentucky. My mom and dad were divorced. I lived in an extended family home with my mother, grandmother, grandfather, aunty, uncle and their kids. I once lived in Japan and in Utah with my father and when we moved to the west end of Louisville, it was a culture shock. It was a different way of life than anything I was ever used too.

When I started school in Louisville, I had the problem of being talkative and never finishing my work. I was always a social butterfly. I had to repeat the third grade and on the second go around, I had a teacher that was really open and understanding. She accepted me for who I was. She taught me how to read poetry and how to dance to it. We had a substitute teacher that used to come to our school who only had one hand. He would always tell us that we could be anything that we wanted to be. During that year, something told me that I would be a teacher, but not just a teacher, an educator as well. Once I got into middle school, I just flourished. I had an awesome principal and teachers who recognized my potential. I am a survivor of violence so I knew that I had some demons that I had to fight but nothing was going to stop me from being an educator.

I teach creative writing at Wheatley Elementary School and am able to work with all grade levels in the school. I don't teach one specific grade. The school is made up of mostly at-risk kids, black and white kids who all face the same reality of poverty. I was named Kentucky's Elementary Teacher of the year in 2018-19. The creating writing that I teach is strictly through hip hop. We study poetry. Last year as we were getting ready for Phillis Wheatley day, one of the poets that we studied was Tupac Shakur. The students made a song about the violence surrounding the community and named the song after one of Tupac's famous known songs, "California Love." The students developed a dance to the song and shot a video. It's very fun to teach because all the kids can relate.

There's a lot of pressure that comes with being a teacher. There's pressure of having to educate someone else's children. There's pressure from other teachers who are always in competition with one another. There is pressure from the community because I feel like our communities still don't treat teachers as professionals. It's hard to live in a society where teachers aren't a concern. Teachers aren't seen as the guiding light as they are. I will tell you that in order to be a successful educator, it has to be your calling. It's a ministry.

Many of my students face significant pressures at home and a majority of them suffer from post-traumatic stress disorder. When they come to school, they have to overcome the struggles from home and the struggles of if they trust the teacher or not. You have to be able to build a foundation based on trust with your students and if not, it's not going to work, especially in urban schools.

One way to build that trust is to have engaging lessons in your classrooms; lessons that are going to interest the kids and allow you to get to know and understand them. If a teacher is getting to school at the same time the kids are getting to school and leaving right when the kids are leaving, you're not giving yourself enough time to build those relationships with your students. I like to go into the cafeteria with them and eat lunch or have them come into the classroom and eat lunch. I've worked on keeping some of my students after school so that we can work on activities together. I sometimes take the kids to the park just to watch them play. I sometimes will call my students when they're at home just to check on them and see what activities they're doing at home.

I am really trying to change lives, but in order for me do that, I feel like I really need to have my hands on my students. My students have my cellphone number; they can text or call me at any time. I like to go and pick them up and take them out for outings and help provide them enough opportunities to help them change their future. I also struggled with that last year because I wore myself thin. I felt like I was trying to do too much. This school year, I will find balance.

I like where education is and where it's headed. I also think that we have a long way to go. I believe that our schools are not child friendly in urban areas. They're child friendly for suburbia schools. Suburbia schools have so much and better technology compared to the urban schools. In the urban schools, the structure inside the school appears to me to be set up almost like a prison. Students are always in uniform. They have to walk in single file lines down the hall.

They can't talk. Those rules and regulations mirror prisons. I understand that some of our kids need to be in structured environments but some of them also need the ability to be free and to be comfortable being a kid inside of the school.

When schooling was first introduced in America, they were set up to provide obedient workers. School shouldn't look like that nowadays. That's one reason I teach on the elements of hip hop. One of the nine elements of hip-hop is entrepreneurship. The students now need to think like an entrepreneur and even if they never become an entrepreneur, they need to have those same qualities of solving problems and learning to get along with people who are different from them. Right now, if you have two kids who believe differently about something, the kids don't know how to compromise because they don't understand how to understand someone else's views.

My advice for teachers going forward is to build relationships with your students. Tomorrow is a new day. Kids are really forgiving. If you mess up one day, don't beat yourself down over it. Kids will forgive you the next day.

I am NyRee Clayton-Taylor I have survived
PRESSURE

Chapter 6

When I was a kid, I used to love watching the Chicago Bulls basketball games whenever they aired locally throughout the area. That was my only chance of getting to watch Michael Jordan play. I loved watching him play just to see the high-flying dunks and the array of moves he put on his opponents.

The Chicago Bulls won many championships in which Jordan received all the credit, but what gets lost in conversations is how clutch his teammates were in pivotal moments. Jordan prepared his teammates to never let the pressure of any game be too big for them.

Basketball is a team sport and Jordan knew in order to win championships, his teammates had to be ready to produce in high-pressure situations.

Playing alongside the best player in the world came with very high expectations. Jordan knew that he would have to count on his teammates because of all the attention he attracted, especially in crucial parts of the game.

At nine years old, I remember watching game six of the 1997 NBA finals like it was yesterday.

Chicago Bulls vs Utah Jazz.

I was sitting Indian style on the floor in our living room glued to the television. The game was tied 86-86 with 25 seconds left and the Bulls had possession of the ball for one final shot. Everyone in the entire world knew who was going to take the last shot for the Bulls.

It is apparent that in the final timeout before play resumed, Jordan told his teammate, Steve Kerr, to be ready to shoot the ball because he knew Utah would double-team him.

Kerr nodded his head and said, "I'll be ready."

Can you imagine the thoughts that probably ran through Steve Kerr's head walking out of that time-out? With a world championship on the line, the greatest player in the world just placed all of the pressure on you. It was also a tough spot for Jordan to be in because if Kerr misses the shot, the entire world, including me, would've been mad at Jordan for passing the ball. No one would've accepted the fact that Jordan was being double-teamed and made the correct basketball play. Everyone would've just remembered the fact that he passed the ball and that whoever took the shot...missed.

Pressure

How many of you would have been ready for that moment under those pressurized circumstances? How many of you would've been prepared to take the biggest shot of your life and have the confidence that you were going to make it? I have played basketball my entire life. I have taken thousands on top of thousands of jump shots and my uncertainty in that moment would've definitely been elevated.

As Jordan started to make his move, Utah brought the double-team and Kerr was left wide open in the center of the court. Jordan willingly passed it off to Kerr and the rest is history. I love that story because it exhibits so many lessons one could take away, all centered around pressure. When you plan and prepare for certain situations, your confidence and ability to execute will outweigh any negative emotions. When you're faced with challenges and you're not prepared, you are more likely to be defeated. The feeling you have emotionally after facing defeat but knowing you could've been more prepared is very disappointing.

Steve Kerr knew that one day he could potentially have to make a huge shot to win a game so from what I've read, he spent countless hours in the gym making game-like shots.

Had he not prepared himself mentally to be reliable in that situation, he would've been too nervous or not ready to deliver in the finals like he did.

When I look back at moments throughout my high school basketball career, I think about how great our team was defensively. We put so much pressure on opposing teams with our full court press and made it really tough for teams to even cross half court...much less score on us. My senior year, we won thirty-three games and only lost three. Only one team in the state of Kentucky defeated us but they defeated us twice. They beat us the first game of the year and the last game of the year.

We were a really good with many talented players. We pressed the entire game and what I mean by "pressed," is we extended our defense the full length of the court to steal the ball from the other team. We ran 80% of the teams that we played out of the gym. What I mean by "ran them out of the gym," is we were winning by so many points that the opposing teams couldn't wait for the game to end and go home.

When we pressed other teams, we knew right away when they were not prepared or just couldn't handle the pressure. The teams that weren't prepared, had

Pressure

guards that dribbled into traps and let us easily steal the ball. Every team that we played already knew that our pressure was fierce and to play us and not be prepared was inexcusable.

Failing to prepare is preparing to FAIL.

Now, let's stop for a minute and think about how other teams not preparing for our pressure and being blown out of the gym relates so much to real life situations.

Have you ever walked into a job interview and knew nothing about the company? How did your interview go? Did you get the job? Do you remember when you were so excited to get your driver's license but feared the parallel parking portion of the test? Did you practice parallel parking before the driving test or did you bump the cones and fail the test because you were winging it? Have you ever failed a test in the classroom because you waited until the night before the test to study? These types of scenarios can be avoided if we decided to not put things off and prepare like there was no tomorrow.

I was watching a YouTube video of an inspirational speaker by the name of Inky Johnson present to an audience about preparing for real life situations and how not preparing can destroy a person. He told a story that really hit home with me. Any spare-time that I have, I like to browse the internet and watch as many inspirational speakers as possible. I take full advantage of being able to learn from the world's best with the easy access of technology.

Inky Johnson is one of my favorite speakers to listen to because he and I have a very similar story. His athletic career was cut short due to injuries and he travels around the country spreading a message about overcoming adversity, much like I do.

In this particular video, Inky shared a story that really put life into perspective. I sometimes share this story when I am speaking in front of crowds.

There was a kid who lived in Atlanta, Georgia, who wasn't particularly doing so well in school and the kid's mother reached out to Inky for some guidance. Inky decided that one day, he would pick the kid up and drive him through downtown Atlanta, to give the kid some perspective. When Inky picked the kid up one afternoon, he took him to a section in the city where homeless people gathered to sleep.

One evening as the homeless individuals were gathering for a night of sleep, Inky and the young man slowly drove by and took in the scene through

Pressure

the window of the car. They spotted a man who was getting ready for sleep.

Inky asked the young man, "Why do you think that man is here preparing for a night of sleep in a card board box? Do you think this was strategic? You think he planned that?"

> The young man said, "no."
> Inky said, "come on, take a shot, what you think happened?"
> The kid said, "I don't know. Tell me what you think happened, Inky?"
> Inky said, "I think life happened. I guarantee you that he had something he wanted. I guarantee somebody told him how great he was. I guarantee you he has a certain skill set. I guarantee you that at a certain point in his life, he was a part of something and he was killing it. But, what he didn't understand was everybody on the face of this planet wants something.

The young man sat quietly in almost disbelief and took in the lesson that Inky was trying to teach him.

Twany Beckham

"Everybody wants to win but everybody doesn't have the will to prepare to win. Everybody just wants the victory." - Inky

I have re-watched that part of the video a thousand times.

I found the story that Inky shared to be really interesting because I once lived in Atlanta and used to drive past that particular section Inky was referencing. I can remember riding by there one night and seeing all of the people sleeping on the side of the curb in cardboard boxes. You have to wonder, where in the world was any of their family members, friends, associates...I mean anybody that could give these folks a roof to lie under. Then you wonder, what in the world did these people do in order to be living under those circumstances.

Is pressure that demoralizing?

Life has many twists and turns. But, one thing that I am going to assure you, is that you and I, or anyone that we're associated with, will never sleep outside in a cardboard box.

Whatever life throws at us, we will be prepared.

Pressure

Throughout my journey, I've been knocked down so many times. I have been presented with so many situations that could have forced me to give up on life. I have faced so many situations that could've crippled me into being dispirited.

But………. I've never QUIT

I will fight until I can't fight any longer. Just adopting that mentality, will give yourself justice.

There have been situations surface in my life that I didn't prepare for; situations that could drive someone crazy. I am sure that you have had situations pop up that have plagued you in your life at some point. The lesson that I have learned, is to never let situations compound into much greater issues. Let's do all that we can to never let life get to a breaking point to where we have to sleep outside in a card board box. Let's prepare our minds to understand that pressure and storms will show face but you have to get up, brush yourself off and keep attacking life.

<u>Pressure made me who I am</u>

Deanna Boone

I take my health so serious at this point in my life. There have been many times in my life where I could've turned to drugs, drinking and many other avenues. I know we're not supposed to ask God "why," but I have asked him what he wants me to do with what he has allowed me to go through. I know he has a reason and I don't know what that reason is right now, but hopefully one day, I will. I have had to endure almost dying, strokes, heart attacks, being attacked sexually, mentally and physically. I almost died with my diabetes like my grandmother. I know God has let me go through all of this to someday be able to help someone. Whether it's helping someone physically or mentally, I want to be that inspiration for others that God has called me to be.

My doctor once told me to lose weight and start eating better. I was hesitant because I love my cupcakes. My doctor let me know that I could have my cupcakes but to cut back some. I did a 360 with my health. I went from a size 14 to a size 6. I eat better. I feel better, but I still have pain. There are new things going on in my life. I have a hole in my heart and I am facing heart surgery. I am facing possible back surgery, but I know God has a plan and he has allowed me every day to get up and say thank you, Jesus.

You don't have to look very far to see somebody that has it a lot worse than you do. That has allowed me to change mentally, spiritually, and physically. It has made me appreciate life that much more because even though it's hard, I can get up and enjoy life. It's a struggle. It's painful, but I don't complain. There are days where I cry and I tell the Lord I'm tired and ask him to give me a reason to keep going. And then someone will come up to me and ask me for prayers.

There are people who go through situations that the world will never see; things like people needing help being bathed or needing help with cutting the water on. Some people will need help for rest of their entire lives with cutting the water on and for those reasons alone, you appreciate life.

We are unbelievably blessed. At our church, we help so many people and organizations, one being the Isiah House. The Isiah House is an organization that helps men that are addicted to drugs, alcohol or just have an addiction to something. They come to our church every Sunday and they fill the pew. At the end of their rehab, most of the men can never go back to where they came from, because if they did, they would relapse. They have these homes that are close to the shelter and they allow for these men to stay there and help them find jobs. It helps them not go back to where they came from, but most importantly, helps them start a new life. Our church went out and purchased tooth brushes, toothpaste, and things that are disposable for most of us. And, those men appreciated that so much. When our church has functions like ice cream parties or fourth of July festivities, all of them come out and they fit in just like normal people. You couldn't tell them differently from any other men that are at the functions. They are great young men who have great testimonies. Some of these men have joined bands, sing gospel music and landed good jobs. God has put people like Twany and I on this earth and blessed us abundantly so that we can go out and help others that are less fortunate.

Someone recently ask me if I regret anything that has happened in my life and I said no. All of the things that have happened to me have opened my eyes and allowed me the strength to be able to help other people. Sometimes I still hurt and sometimes I go into a stage of depression that people don't outwardly see but its inwardly felt by me. I occasionally have bad days to where I sometimes cry out to the Lord for relief. If you looked at me you would never see me as anyone that could be depressed. I keep it inside of me because I am someone who wants to be strong for others.

How I handle the pressures of everyday life is, I remind myself every day that God is in control. You don't have to look very far to see someone that has it way worse than you do. I live by the Bible and by my faith. I can sing gospel music for hours. That's my happy place. God is not done with me yet. I will leave you with my favorite bible verse.

Isaiah 40-31

But those who hope in the Lord
Will renew their strength.
They will soar on wings like eagles.
They will run and not grow weary.
They shall walk and not be faint.

I am Deanna Boone and I have survived PRESSURE.

Interlude Two

Have you figured out by now that hardly anyone is doing what they envisioned doing when they were a little kid? Have you figured out by now that living a stress-free life is almost impossible? Do you remember the times when you first started envisioning how you wanted your life to be? Do you remember how many times you've had to answer the question "what do you want to be when you grow up?" Can you remember some of the answers that you've uttered?

Whether you were sitting in a classroom answering your teachers or answering family members at holiday gatherings, you've always came face to face with this question.

In one sense, it was a great question to be asked because it made you outwardly express your dreams and create expectations for yourself. However, it created large amounts of pressure for you. Some of us knew and understood exactly what our dreams and aspirations were but there were others who had no idea what they wanted to be and just threw things out there.

Pressure

The unprepared typically throw out the first few lavish jobs or lifestyles that pop into their heads. I have witnessed this so many times. I remember one specific time being asked this question by my 5th grade teacher. One of my friends blurted out that he wanted to be a chemical engineer. I looked at my friend with the "you don't even know what a chemical engineer is," face.

I am not here to judge anyone because I sometimes found myself in the group that when asked that question, said anything that sounded good. I can remember telling teachers that I was going to be the next big NBA superstar. I've even yelled out movie star and even told people that I was going to be a millionaire by the time I was twenty-one years old.

Take a second and think about where you are in life and if you envisioned being in this particular spot. If you are living out your dreams, take a second and be thankful for everything you've had to endure to make that possible. If you are doing something that you totally didn't dream of, or think you would be doing, but love what you're doing, take a second and be thankful for everything you've had to endure to make that possible.

If you are not where you want to be in life and are struggling to find a passion and love for something, don't worry, it's never too late. You can also take a second to be thankful and appreciate these times as well.

Your time is coming...stay patient.

Finding a passion in life puts so much pressure on you but when you break through, the feeling is unimaginable. Everything that you went through to reach that point all makes sense.

Over the years, I have come to a happy medium with learning how to alleviate placing pressure on my future and it has worked for me. Whenever I get asked the questions "what are your future plans, or where do you see yourself in years to come"? I have eluded to.... "Wherever God takes me."

I've tried to predict the outcome of my future and have tried to place myself in situations that I thought would help maximize my attempts at reaching goals. In my life, nothing has ever gone as planned. I've learned that it's always good to be proactive and to control as much of your life as you can, but being reactive pays its dividends as well.

Pressure

I've done nothing extravagant but follow God's plan for my life and it's beautiful watching the pieces of the puzzle come together.

Chapter 7

My entire life has been predicated on performing, whether it was performing well in the classroom or on the basketball court, I've had to meet expectations to advance my life. I absolutely love it. I love having to perform, especially when the stage is big and the lights are the brightest. I love competing. I love showing off my skills and how hard I've worked. I love the feeling of simply being challenged. That's the competitive nature in me. I've always approached life as if I was the underdog and I believe embracing that mentality has helped me when having to perform. I always feel like I have something to prove and I thrive off proving people wrong.

I believe that in all facets of life, you have to perform well at some points in order to advance at doing anything. This is pressure showing its face in another form.

When I think about someone who had to perform at the highest level under serious pressure, I think about the greatest boxer of all time, Muhammad Ali. He had to perform exceedingly well every time he stepped in the ring because of all the pressure he placed on himself. Muhammad Ali loved to guarantee victory and humorously mock his opponents before the fight. Not only did Ali place the pressure on himself of having to win the fight, he went as far as predicting the exact round that he would knock out his opponent. And, he very seldom under delivered on his promises.

I've never let the pressure to perform get the best of me. I have always reverse engineered the fear that comes with performing and used it as fuel in my beliefs of opportunities. I am one who has learned to never take opportunities for granted. You never know when an opportunity will come back around...if ever.

For instance, if your job required you to give presentations and you don't give each presentation your all, you essentially could miss out on an opportunity that can change your life. It could be that one presentation that you didn't fully prepare for that could come back to bite you.

Blowing an opportunity can be as simple as botching a Friday afternoon presentation because it's Friday and because your mind is already on weekend mode. Well, what you don't know is that person who could potentially be your next employer is going to be attending your presentation. You casually go through your presentation and the energy in which you present was significantly lower than usual. Now, you've unimpressed someone in the room that could have held the keys to your future. Blowing an opportunity can be that simple.

The goal should be to prepare as if your life relied on this presentation and control what you can control- YOUR ATTITUDE and EFFORT.

If you had known that your next employer was going to attend your presentation, how would you have prepared to perform?

From 2010 to 2013, I had the pleasure of being coached by Hall of Fame Coach, John Calipari. I had the indulgence of seeing a coach who loved to perform at the highest of highest levels; and, a coach who expected the same day-to-day performance out of his players.

At that point in my career, the NBA was a long shot for me but I practiced and pushed my younger teammates as if I was NBA bound too. I brought my A-game every single day of practice, which in return helped make my younger teammates better.

Pressure

The process also involved bringing a group of five-star freshman together in order to achieve one goal. If we win like we were expected too, everyone would essentially reach their goals in the end. For Coach Cal, this was a year in and year out thing for him.

On a yearly basis, Coach Cal has to take the youngest team in college basketball and compete for a championship at a school that is expected to win every game...YES, every game.

The pressure to perform for these eighteen and nineteen-year-old kids, start in the classroom and then onto the basketball court. Universally, we all understand that you have to be successful in the classroom in order to even step foot in a collegiate athletic setting. There were times throughout my college career where I didn't know how I managed to do both.

In order to become the best version of myself, I always needed to put in extreme work on the court and in the weight room. My jump shot has basically needed work from the time I started playing basketball, so I spent countless of hours in the gym, working on it. The physicality of college sports requires you to get stronger or it will be hard for the average person to compete, so I always worked on strengthening my body.

One thing that couldn't go without notice and was the most important out of everything was my school work. Balancing athletics and academics in college has its degree of difficulty. Let me give you an example….

We have a Tuesday night, ESPN, 9 o'clock primetime game against the University of Florida at their place. The game, depending on how it's officiated, should be over at approximately 11:00 p.m. After the game, the team has to fulfill media responsibilities and then catch a flight back home. Let's just say, we arrive home safely between 1:00 and 1:30 a.m. and you have a test in Biology 101 at 8:00 a.m. You're probably wondering how anyone could be ready to take a test at the crack of dawn after that type of schedule.

For the younger guys on the team, this type of scheduling could be challenging, especially for the players who logged thirty plus minutes in the game. The last thing on a player's mind when arriving back home would be studying for a test.

Pressure

I had already gone through the gauntlet the previous two years of college, so I was seasoned. How I approached scenarios like this was simple. I studied days and days ahead knowing that this type of scenario would come up. I would take my books on the road with me and study whenever we had down time in the hotel. Even though this sounded like a fix to the situation, I bet it was still tough on the guys who played all the minutes and even harder if you are getting in bed in the middle of the night after a loss. That would make it that much harder to mentally prepare for a test the next morning.

Pressure made me who I am

Kyle Wiltjer

The reason I decided to go to Kentucky was to make myself a better player and to push myself to uncomfortable limits. I had a lot of people telling me to go to one of the local schools where I grew up like Oregon or Gonzaga in order to be sure that I'd play. People didn't realize that I was a McDonald's All-American myself so I felt like I didn't have to settle. I wanted to go play with the best players in the country.

When I arrived at Kentucky, I thought that there was going to be this enormous amount of pressure to succeed. In which there is because of the fans, 24,000 on hand at every game who expected us to win every game. But, when you actually touch down in Kentucky, Coach Calipari and his staff take the pressure out of it. They make you feel like family and all you do is work. There is no time to sit around and think about the pressure.

Every single day, our goal was to just get through that day. You hit the weights, you have individual workouts, you have practice, all on top of going to class half the day. The toughest part out of everything was the going and staying focused in the classroom. In the midst of everything, our team developed such a brotherhood. Even though each guy was working extremely hard, it still felt like you were working with your brothers.

When we won the National Championship in 2012, we rolled through the season because we all got lost in working our tails off and wanting to win for each other. That took the pressure out of it. I can remember hitting two huge threes in the Final Four games against Louisville. My friends back at home all were asking me how nervous I was to play in that game. I had to tell them I had

Pressure

no nervous energy because at that point, it was about performing like I had performed all year. You fast forward to the second year, and that's where the pressure set in because we set the bar so high the previous year. It was tough for me because, we had five players leave for the NBA after the first year and I was still in school having to live off of a scholarship check. That's when real life hit me. When you can't fill up your gas tank, comfortably pay for a meal at a nice restaurant but your boys who you played with a year ago are buying Range Rovers and huge houses, that is very humbling. But, it made me go work even harder. I also had the pressure of having to mix in with the new five-star players that Kentucky brought in. My role wasn't guaranteed. I had to prove myself all over again.

After my sophomore season at Kentucky, and with the help of Coach Calipari, I transferred to the University of Gonzaga. I needed that move for my career because I wanted to prove my worth with more pressure being added on my shoulders. At Gonzaga, I knew that I would be one of the main guys. The benefit of playing at Kentucky was you had other five star players to pick you up if you were playing bad. At Gonzaga, if I played bad, we lost. I needed that pressure for my personal development. Everyone's story is different. I ended up staying in school for five years and just like Twany, I knew that basketball was going to stop at some point. So, for me, it was vitally important that I also finish school in a part of the country that I will more than likely be working when basketball is over. No one in my family had a college degree, so I wanted to take that pressure off my family as well.

I always assumed that people viewed me as a really smart kid, but I was the complete opposite. School was a struggle for me. There was hardly any time to do school. Think about this – we have two practices a day, classes in between, you have to make sure to feed yourself and stay hydrated. When you get home at night, the last thing I wanted to do was open a book. At Gonzaga, I was studying business and you had to maintain a 3.0 GPA. On top of my basketball schedule, I had to put in some serious work and effort. There were points in my life where I questioned if I could make it through to get my degree. I was able to get two degrees, but I can't honestly tell you how in the world I managed to do it.

The pressure in different life situations is always going to be there, but for me, the trick is acting like it isn't there. The key for me is STAYING IN YOUR LANE. You can't worry about what anyone else is doing or where anyone else is in life. I am a late bloomer. When I first got to Kentucky, I had a ton of baby fat. I was working out four and five times a day, so it wasn't because I wasn't working hard. I have a different development. I couldn't go in every year worrying about how strong any of my teammates were, I just worried about increasing my levels. Right now, I am the best version of myself. I might not be jumping out of the gym, but I do what I do very well and that's how life has got me to where I'm at.

I am Kyle Wiltjer and I have survived PRESSURE.

I have a friend name Brett Berry that has been in my life since the 6th grade. His family were some of the first people to show me life outside of where I grew up. They lived on a golf course in what I would consider a mansion, compared to any apartment I had ever lived in. They had a basketball court in the driveway so you know where Brett and I spent most of our time outside of playing video games.

Brett and I became like brothers and his family is like a second family to me. Brett just recently asked me to be a groomsman in his wedding and I couldn't be more elated.

Brett and I talk on the phone often, and a conversation we had recently, really put some things into perspective for me. I've always had an idea of how stressful going through law school was, but I didn't realize how much pressure it was to officially become a lawyer.

After you graduate from law school, you have to perform well on the "bar exam," in order to practice law. You can go through several years of law school and make unbelievable grades, but none of that matters if you can't pass the "bar exam."

Brett and I were catching up on the phone, as we usually do, asking each other how our lives were going etc. I usually have the same answer whenever Brett and I catch up.

> "I'm doing good, Brett, just working hard as ever trying to make a way." Brett responded with, "same man, but I am studying like crazy so I can try to pass this test."

I am a real inquisitive person, so I asked Brett about the hours he spent studying and what the implications were if he didn't pass the test. He informed me that the bar was only given two times a year and if he failed to pass it, he'll more than likely be in the market for another job for the time-being. My mind cringed for him.

With the test only being available to take twice a year and having to pay money to even take it, can you imagine the pressure that had to have on someone? Knowing you can't go forward with your career until you pass the test. It reminded me of the feeling I felt when I had to pass the ACT test in order to get into college. Brett said that the pressure of taking the bar is indescribable. He said the hardest thing about studying for the bar is the isolation.

> *"Unless you're studying with other law students, you are by yourself for hours on top of hours studying. You can't really tell people what you're feeling. It is the hardest emotions that I have ever dealt with. It's paralyzing."*
> Brett

Take a second to reflect on your daily behaviors. Are you under constant pressure to perform? If you are, how are you performing? Are you satisfied with your performance? Could you improve? Have you had to make any adjustments in order to get different or better results?

Pressure made me who I am

Jazzmar Ferguson

You know the days where you have no desire to roll out of bed and be productive: body tired, feet sore, mentality drained. I have experienced many of those days within the past seven years, which only leads me to believe that I will have more days and nights similar to those, in the future.

The unusual reality about those kinds of days for me is that they tend to be my best days to counter those challenging desires of taking an extra day off or postponing cardio for a later occasion in the week. Instead, pushes me to wake up, hit the weight room, and head to the gym to fine tune my skills and strengthen my weaknesses.

The dedication and desire to maintain a certain standard at the pro basketball level will certainly challenge you. When you have your best days physically, mentally and emotionally, it's easy to sustain the motivation required to meet the high-performance expectations. But, when you are able to meet those same expectations when your level of energy doesn't cause for greatness, you are preparing for a much bigger purpose.

Pressure

Pressure is an aspect of life that you have to be mentally prepared to resist against. In my case, the pressure to perform on the big stage comes just about every Sunday evening from October to May.

I have been fortunate enough to play professional basketball abroad in three amazing countries. My career started in Canada. It was a brief stint... three months or so, but a very eye-opening experience. Seeing a total of 13 players being cut from their duties of that particular team in a matter of weeks, or days in some cases, taught me that if you don't have the ability to perform under pressure, your job, career and livelihood could be at stake every night.

My brief stint in Canada enabled my mind to completely embrace the fact that I was very fortunate to be playing this game I dearly love, but also it helped me grow an even bigger desire to prove myself. This opportunity was presented in Australia. Understanding the very low expectations my first team in Australia expressed, we completely exceeded that and won a championship. With that, came numerous "big games," important in-game situations and pressure filled action! My second year in Australia was much more of the same. Though, we didn't win a championship the next year, I had developed a reputation as a guy who was reliable in the clutch moments of the games, which allowed me to further my career. Opportunities presented themselves overnight it seems, which ultimately lead to the longest thirty-two hours of my life...Melbourne to Singapore...Singapore to Paris...Paris to Bologna.

When I arrived in Pasta Land, there was a major culture shock. I was completely out of my comfort zone. The language barrier was immediately a burden. My team who essentially "took a chance" on me, by giving me an opportunity to make the difficult transition from a lower level market outside of the premium European standards, was highly criticized for signing an undersized combo guard, who was unproven in Europe. Understanding how the business of the sport is orchestrated, critics had good reason to raise eyebrows. But, with all of the head scratching...negative thoughts going through everyone's heads. The guy who had everything to gain and everything to lose, was prepared for the level of competition; the beating of drums and the chants that those passionate fans roar from start to finish; for the big moments in close games; for the doubters; and the everyday challenges to communicate with

people who didn't speak the same language. I was always prepared, for the pressure.
As I humbly state that I will now be entering the eighth year of my professional career, I will proudly be returning to Italy for a sixth consecutive year.

Since I was a skinny seven-year-old with very limited skills, I've always loved the game of basketball. Many of my friends growing up in the low income downtown Louisville area were great athletes. For those of us who played organized basketball, I was certainly the least skilled, and the smallest, but my mind wouldn't allow me to accept not being good enough. I understood at eleven years old that if I didn't improve my skills every single day, then I would probably never have the ability to play organized basketball (middle school, high school, college etc.). So, I dedicated my life to this beautiful game...mentally, physically and emotionally, day and night. I pushed myself to the absolute limit every single day as a teenager. Lifting weights to get stronger, running cross country to increase my endurance, and most importantly, I used the thought of not being able to play to motivate me intellectually. Yes, this game helped me get through every phase of school academically.

Michele Carrea, my former coach at Pallacanestro Biella once told me that my greatest skill as a player was my mentality. That statement was likely the greatest compliment I have ever received, because I know that I would not be living my dream in this time of my life without having the ability to prepare for the pressure.

Mentally, always understand that if you are not motivated to do your job or willing to sustain the level of expectation in which you are expected to fulfill, then you can be replaced.

Physically, do what is necessary to prepare your body for long, grueling seasons. Lift weights, train to improve your skills, maintain a healthy and disciplined diet. And always find time to rest when your body needs it. LISTEN TO YOUR BODY.

Emotionally, remain even keel. The highs are never as high as they seem, the lows are never as low. With a balanced emotional approach, the mind and body follow suit.

    I am Jazzmar Ferguson and I have survived PRESSURE.

Chapter 8

Have you ever had a time in your life where you wondered if your existence was good enough for the world we live in, or if people would accept you the way that you are?

Do you often find yourself changing your behavior or the way you present yourself because you want to be accepted? If you do, don't worry; you are not alone. Many people in our society struggle with this daily and I have been one of those people…and sometimes still am.

Acceptance can be looked upon as both positive and negative depending on the particular situation. Let's say that you find people wearing hoodies in 100-degree weather totally fine because you can relate with such actions. The majority of people will deem those actions as being different or weird, especially if they can't relate.

Have you ever been in someone's home who doesn't have window treatment on their windows and are very comfortable going to bed in that type of setting? That would make me extremely uncomfortable. I am dumbfounded as to how people do it. But, again, I couldn't relate. The way I grew up, closing every blind...locking every car and house door wasn't debatable.

Merriam-Webster defines acceptance as "the quality or state of being accepted or acceptable. That's clear, cut, dry and to the point, right?

We live in a society where there is so much freedom of expression and individuals have the right to be whoever they want to be. On the flip side, our society is extremely judgmental and people have a hard time accepting things that they aren't used too.

Think about the things and people that you don't accept or agree with. Have you ever taken a second to sit and think about why you don't actually accept this person or their actions? If you haven't, I encourage you to do so.

Get out a piece of paper and jot down five people or things that you don't necessarily accept and explain why? I did this and found that I really didn't have reasons for some of the things or people I didn't accept? I can almost guarantee that the majority of you will come across similar feelings.

From the time you were born, you've had an uphill battle with acceptance. Based on your ethnicity, race, or socio-economic class, you've had to deal with different levels of pressure with being accepted. There are some people in the world who look at everyone the same without judgement, but that's a tough reality for everyone to associate with.

I was born African American and I can't do anything about that. I can't do anything about where and how I was raised. All I ever wanted was to be viewed in the same light as everyone else...as far as society accepting my existence as normal and with equality.

I wanted to be embraced like a normal kid. I wanted to be liked by all of the kids at the predominately white elementary school that I attended from the third through fifth grade. I wanted the luxury of sitting down at the lunch table with the white kids and they not get up and move. I wanted the chance to interact with kids from suburban neighborhoods and hear stories about them playing basketball in their back yards and swimming in their pools. Even though I couldn't relate and didn't grow up like some of my classmates, I found their stories motivational. I started visualizing my kids growing up with those experiences one day.

I was born and raised in an area where we are labeled as project kids...thugs and hoodlums. The chances of being accepted outside of where I grew up are almost slim to none. Some of us never come close to having the opportunity to be accepted outside of the projects because for some, opportunities to leave the area are never presented.

How are we supposed to find opportunity when we don't know that those certain opportunities exist? If you have no idea about the resources that are available, then how can one seek information and help? It seems as if people from impoverished communities live with blinders on and are oblivious to the whole world outside of the projects.

I've had to fight battles to let people know that kids from the projects aren't always made out to be what they try to make us out to be. If given more chances at being accepted for whom we are as people and not how we look or where we come from, I think the paradigm will shift. I'm hopeful.

Where I come from made it difficult throughout the early years of my life to be accepted. As I've mentioned, I was a really good athlete and a kid who wanted to do something positive with my life.

Pressure

To be different and have your own identity living in the projects wasn't an easy thing to do. That in itself was pressure, both good and bad.

I used to get into pointless fights with other kids in the neighborhood and steal from the neighborhood candy store just because I saw other kids doing it. I've thrown rocks at windows and knocked on neighbor's doors in the middle of the night. My mother didn't raise me to do any of these things, but I had a group of friends in the neighborhood that I wanted to be accepted by. I wanted to feel like I was a part of the "crew."

There was one incident in the midst of me running around with the "crew," that really scared me and had me second guessing if this was really the life I wanted. One afternoon, a couple of us from my neighborhood got on the bus that took us to a mall in Indiana. We had plans to go into a store that sold BB guns...steal them and run out. In doing so, a police officer who was monitoring the area spotted our suspicious activity and came running after us. I can remember running through a parking lot ducking behind car after car. Instead of sticking together, we all ran completely separate ways. Fortunately, I was able to get away and get on a bus headed back to my neighborhood. Several of my friends got caught and detained by the police.

I had never experienced anything like that in my life. All I could think about was the spanking I would get if my mother found out what happened. Hold up... let me rephrase that...the beating I would get.

When I arrived home, I hugged my mother with a sigh of relief. I never actually told her what happened and was glad she wasn't too inquisitive about my day. The crazy thing about this was my family isn't really intimate with one another. We rarely hug. So, for me to hug my mother when I came in the house definitely raised red flags.

Growing up in an area where the most successful people were those who made money illegally, was always hard for kids like me. Those people were the ones who we looked up too for motivation. They were the people who were accepted and loved in my community. They drove the nicest cars and had the latest fashion. Their lifestyles weren't easy to ignore.

I never wanted to follow in those exact same footsteps, but it was hard to see those material possessions and not be intrigued. We could be

Pressure

playing basketball in the community park and see a souped-up car drive by and immediately be inspired.

 As a kid growing up with pretty much nothing, how could you not want those types of possessions and not feel like you needed to have it in order to be "cool." When I put myself in their shoes, I can see how one could catch a buzz from the thought of motivating the kids in the neighborhood.

 I have always been comfortable in my own skin. My body being covered in tattoos has never made me uncomfortable because tattoos are a part of the basketball culture. Now that I am in the real world and outside of the whole sports sphere, having tattoos all over my body has become a pressure. I'm always self-conscious about them. I love who I am and have no regrets with the artwork covering my body but you can't control how others view you.

When I go and speak to kids, especially the ones who aspire to be professional athletes, I proudly show my tattoos because those kids can relate to that. Every athlete that these kids see on the Television screen, looks just like me.

When I give presentations in professional settings, I make sure to dress in long sleeve shirts just to cover up my tattoos. I try to avoid any judgement and strive for people to give me the same attention they would anyone else. Since I have grown to be very confident and comfortable with whom I am as a person, my tattoos don't bother me as much anymore. Having tattoos doesn't diminish the fact that I am an educated man who is very passionate about my career in helping and inspiring people.

Having tattoos is just a way that I express myself and people shouldn't be looked at any lesser of a person because of them.

A kid that I grew up with was kicked out of every school that he ever attended. Everyone used to make fun of this kid because he could never finish a school year because of his behavioral issues. One day he and I were playing basketball together in the neighborhood and his mother called him in to take his medicine. The next time I saw him, I can remember asking him what he took medicine for and he disclosed to me a condition that he had and if he didn't take medication, he couldn't be controlled. My perspective about him changed that day. I couldn't understand how one would not be able to control their actions, but there are conditions people have that makes this is a real problem. I say all that to say,

NEVER JUDGE ONES ACTIONS WITHOUT UNDERSTANDING THEIR SITUATION.

Now, in no way, shape or form will I ever condemn people acting stupidly. Instead, I now have the mindset of trying to find out why instead of judging them right away.

Once upon a time in our society the LGBTQ community was not accepted and now they have the rights at the federal level to be married in any state in the United States. The LGBTQ community is creating a wave for themselves along with many others who are working towards an equitable community. How does that make you feel? Are you one to disapprove of the LGBTQ community or have you accepted that it has become a norm to see two men or two women affectionate with one another in a public setting?

I can't even imagine the amount of pressure and stress that is placed on people within the LGBTQ community to live normal and happy lives. Living happily consists of being open with who you are and not caring about the opinions of others. However, that's easier said than done. I read a story one time where a little boy hid who he was his entire life and then committed suicide because the pressure became too much for him. He was afraid to reveal that he was homosexual because he knew his family would not have accepted him. The little boy would rather take his own life than to face the backlash he would receive from his family.

At the end of the day, you have to love who God made you to be and not how others view you. Trust me; I know it's hard to live in your truth at times. It's hard to be completely comfortable in your own skin. Everyone wants to be liked by everyone, but that's an impossible fate. If you love yourself and trust that God made you all to be special in your own way, being socially accepted will be one of the lesser worries in your life.

Are you comfortable in your own skin? Are you holding back from living in your truths? What's holding you back? An opinion? A friend or family member that isn't comfortable in their own skin?

Don't waste another day or another second. Knock down that pressure and LIVE YOUR LIFE

The world we live in and especially the current times have made it tough on the different races in America and all throughout the world. Racism has been an issue for many years and right now every other news story involves it. Many problems can arise with one being an African American but the same thing can be said for other races as well. As my exposure has grown over the years, the group of individuals I've been able to empathize with very closely are those who are bi-racial.

Below you will find perspectives from two bi-racial sisters who I have known for many years. They are both like my little sisters. They come from the same household but have two completely different perspectives on the pressures that they've faced with being bi-racial...

Pressure made me who I am

Asia Poore

I felt like I had a hard time being accepted when I was growing up. My mother is white and my dad is African American, which makes me bi-racial. I was so indecisive about which side I wanted to take and was most comfortable with. I grew up in a suburban neighborhood around all white families so that's who I felt most comfortable around. I wanted to have blue eyes and blonde hair just like the little typical white girl.

Around the 6th and 7th grade, I attended a predominately white school, and that's when I really first started to notice that people looked at me differently. I had a lot of pressure to fit in with my peers at school because there weren't many there that were like me. Walking through the hallways of my schools has always been a struggle for me. I have heard other girls make racial comments outwardly towards me that were very inappropriate. I have been called the "N" word numerous times. That is what has stuck in my head and bothered me the most. It's been really hard for me to get over. But, as I've grown up, I have realized that you just have to push through and embrace the beauty of your race and ethnicity. I still struggle some with people giving me weird looks when I am out in public. I've had people try to tell me how to dress or want me to act a certain way and I have learned to ignore it.

To overcome the pressure of being bi-racial, I have started hanging around people like me, a lot of bi-racial people. I find that I love to interact more with black people because I think that they are a lot like me as well. If this was a perfect world, and I had my choice of a perfect circle of friends, I would have a mixture of black and white people.

I have started having role models that were the same ethnicity as me, so I have become more acceptable with realizing who I am and wanting to connect more with my ethnicity. I inspire to be just like them and love myself for who I am. I don't really care anymore about what race I am or what color my skin is. I feel like I am the same as everyone else. I feel that there shouldn't be a color to you. We should all be equal as one.

For all of you bi-racial people out there or people of other ethnicities, if you hear racial comments being aimed at you, just ignore it and understand the beauty of who you are and the way that you were made. There is no dominancy between races. There is not one that's better than the other. We're all equal. Today, I view myself as a black woman and I am perfectly fine with that!!

I am Asia Poore and I have survived
PRESSURE.

<u>**Pressure made me who I am**</u>

Sydney Poore

Growing up, I identified myself as a white girl. I wanted the blonde hair, blue eye look so that I could look like everyone else. I grew up in a white school, a white community, and I was one of the few bi-racial kids, if not the only one in my school. I had very little interactions with other bi-racial or black kids. I identified mostly with the kids who wore the preppy clothes. I wanted my hair to be blond. I loved to listen to pop music. I never really payed attention to my African American side.

I think growing up with my mom and living in a predominately-white community definitely shaped me to be who I am. I have been able to see what my family that lives in the west end of Louisville, KY goes through, and it's the total opposite of my struggles. I have other bi-racial cousins who live there and their lives are completely different than mine. We like different things, we do different things, and we also view things differently. My dad who is African American has a completely different perspective on life than I have. He believes that if you want to be successful, you have to work hard on your own for everything you desire, because nothing will be handed to you. Whereas for me, I learned that it was ok to be handed things and that it was ok to receive help from others.

I feel like I struggled more with the pressures of being bi-racial when I was younger. People used to make negatives comments towards me all the time. I can remember getting into some altercations because kids didn't like me because of my skin being darker. As I've gotten older, I think times changed and more bi-racial kids are in my classes. I have started embracing who I am. I love to wear my curly hair. I've gotten into wearing makeup and letting myself know that I am beautiful. I listen to other genres of music. I have role models unlike the ones I had growing up. I have gotten closer with my dad's side of my family and I think that has helped me embrace who I am more too.

I feel like I have beaten the pressure of being bi-racial. I have really let go and fell in love with who I am. I don't struggle with it anymore. I don't pay attention to it anymore. I feel beautiful every day.

I am Sydney Poore and I have survived PRESSURE.

Chapter 9

Is the foundation of your goals, dreams and aspirations...money? What I mean by foundation is, where does your motivation come from? What inspires you every single day to chase your goals? If someone had to water the roots of your plants, what type of roots would they be watering?

Are you fueled by putting your time and energy into something that might have the chance of making you rich? What plans would you have to maintain your riches? Do you think being rich will result in you being joyful, and are you built for everything that comes with having riches?

At a young age, I had an experience that opened my eyes to a feeling that only money could have provided. Helping your mother relieve a little pressure by paying a bill has to be one of the best feelings in the world.

The summer heading into my 6th grade year, some of my friends and I were approached by a man in the neighborhood, and he asked us if we were interested in making some money. I saw him around before, but I didn't know exactly who he was. Of course, we all answered...yes, as this guy started to give us his pitch. We were vulnerable. Well, at least I was. He pledged to show us how to make $20 dollars from a box of M&Ms that had 10 single packs in it. The man told us that we could make however much money we wanted. Our take home pay was all dependent on how many boxes of M&Ms that we could sell.

My friends and I thought, man, we can make at least $100 dollars a week and for the first time of my life I could actually have some significant spending money of my own. I didn't run this opportunity past my mother because I already knew what her answer would've been.

The very next day, there we were...on the corner of a busy intersection, with a box of M&M's, approaching businessmen as they casually walked past. I thought this man was some type of genius or something. Those boxes of M&M's were selling like hot cakes. The pack of M&M's were small, but we were told to ask for $2 dollars per pack, which didn't seem to be a problem.

I would sell three and four boxes a day and go home with a pocket full of money. I hid the money from my mother because I didn't want her to put a stop to my hustle. One night, I overheard my mom venting to someone on the phone about needing some cash for a bill, so I decided to lay some money on her bed. She looked at me like I was crazy, but didn't decline the help. That feeling may have been one of the greatest feelings in the world and from that moment on, I wanted to feel that many more times.

It does not get any better than being able to help out your mother. I felt the feeling of what having money can do for you and a little sense of how it could alleviate a little pressure.

The sole purpose of wanting to go to the NBA for me was so that I could become rich and help take care of my family. At times, I still think about how differently life would be had I made it to the NBA, but in another breath, I thank God for not blessing me with those opportunities and opening my mind to many other things.

Coming into millions of dollars in my early 20s would've been tough on me. Mentally, it would've been challenging. At that time in my life, I didn't fully understand how money worked. No one ever taught me. I can only imagine the pressure I would've faced and all the people that would have befriended me for the wrong reason. I wonder how many people would've made me feel guilty for their problems and give me every reason in the world to lend them money. These are real pressures that I've faced without being a millionaire, so I can only imagine what the pressure would've been like if I was.

I could see the positives of becoming a millionaire in my early 20s as well. I could've had a head start on some of the things I dream to accomplish. I would've wanted to change the trajectory of my entire family. I would've used every penny I had to provide opportunity for the underprivileged, and donated heavily to non-profit organizations with those missions. I would've taken my family and friends on trips all around the world to experience adventures that were uncommon to them. I would've bought my mother her dream home and made sure that my two little brothers didn't have a care in the world.

As you can see, having riches would've had its pros and cons for me but the truth of it all is that I wanted to be rich for everyone and everything except for MYSELF. I thought that being rich would validate my existence and have me feeling like I was on top of the world.

I have grown to realize and understand that having money isn't the only real riches that we should strive for.

Joy and happiness are the keys to experiencing real riches.

I have learned to love what I've been blessed with. I've learned to love my family the way that they are, the houses they live in, the clothes they wear, and the times we spend together. I have learned to love my job, the car that I drive, the clothes that I wear and to appreciate every single dollar that my hard work enables me to make. I may not be one of the richest people in the world but the path life is taking me down, has me feeling wholesome.

My purpose in life is to provide hope, inspiration and opportunities to others, but the foundation in which I'm able to fulfill that purpose has changed. I've had to go back and replant my seeds and make sure that as those seeds continue to grow and develop, to always remember why I replanted them.

I've prayed for love and continuous strength along this new journey. I wanted to trust God's timing and believe what was meant for me shall come. I wanted to feel self-love and love from others not dependent on my financial status. I no longer want riches in order to seek validation or to fund personal needs of others or for materialistic pleasures. I want riches so that I can say yes to things that will make the world a better place. I would love to have contributions on implementing educational tools for kids in low poverty areas. I would love to provide resources for adults who struggle to find jobs and offer trainings for skill development.

Trust me, I understand that everyone is different, and the thoughts surrounding money are subjective. You take a person like me, who cherished the thought of being rich so that I could help my family and live a lavish lifestyle, and then you meet a person who is homeless and all he is thankful for is waking up each day…. makes you wonder. They say, "the love of money is the root of all evil." Do you believe that? If so, why?

In my opinion, "the love of money is the root of all evil," can be viewed as subjective…depending on the circumstance. However, what I do believe to be factual is that money can cause people to act very strangely.

I think that when people run into issues or pressures, they think money automatically fixes the problem. And with that mentality, people will do whatever to get it. I've heard of people staging car wrecks so that they can file a claim for insurance money. There are individuals out here that will stage the murder of their significant other to claim the insurance money as well.

Think about the marriages that fall apart. The main pressure surrounding that divorce will be who is getting what from a financial perspective. Think about the people who distribute drugs and put their lives on the line every single day. I have friends who have been killed in drugs deals gone bad and friends who are doing life sentences in prison cells for the chase of money.

My family has never been fortunate to live comfortably financially. We've never experienced the feeling of what having money feels like. We've had to appreciate every win that we could get. Paying the bills on time from month to month and my mother having a reliable car to make it to our little league sports games were huge wins for us. My brothers and I loved cereal when we were kids, and my mother always made sure that we each had our favorite cereal for morning breakfast. Something that small you may think isn't a win but when I reflect on things that made us happy, that was actually a huge win. Every now and then if my brothers and I were lucky, we got a pair of Michael Jordan shoes to wear. As long as we had sports, friends, food and a place to lay our head at night, life was good in the projects.

Pressure

This is why I replanted my seeds and reconstructed my foundation. Some of the happiest times in my life came in the midst of being poor and not having hardly anything. I sometimes search for the periods of my life that made me lose that perspective.

When did my mind shift to me thinking that I needed to be rich in order to be happy and to feel whole? When did I start to feel like I needed money to validate my existence? Why did I feel like I needed to drive the nicest looking car and pay a huge car payment when I really couldn't afford it?

I have wanted to figure out what exactly changed me so that I could stay far away, from whatever it was.

My experiences along this journey have opened my eyes to so much and my perspective has shifted many times. I am still that same person that appreciates growing up in public housing or simply having my favorite box of cereal in the mornings for breakfast. I am still that same person that appreciates not always being able to have everything I wanted as a kid. What makes those times so significant in my life was because I know my mother worked her tail off to afford anything that we ever had. Being able to afford many of the lavish things in life without any pressure was always a dream of mine but not sure if I ever felt like it could be a reality. Our situation was what it was. I didn't know anyone on a personal level who made it out of the projects and got rid of the pressure of not having money.

I want to be that example. I want to show generations after me that it is POSSIBLE!

Pressure made me who I am

Corey Shane Taylor

Success at one point to me strictly meant financial freedom. I believe that was partly because of my upbringing, my cultural influences, and really just how I perceived the world. That is what fueled me for the majority of my journey in Atlanta. It was revealed quickly to me how unstable having that type of motivation was and how unsustainable that type of focus is. At some point, you're going to get the money but if you're not fulfilled, you're going to run out of reasons to wake up and to move up.

My journey started with that realization, and once I tapped out of reasons to get up in the morning, and to outwork everyone around me, and to put passion into each day, I had to take some time for myself to really try to understand what it was that I really wanted out of life. I was able to travel and see the world for the first time, and there I began to realize that my gift was about who I'm serving. It wasn't about my gifts serving me.

The biggest changes that I have made in my life has definitely been going from preaching to people about what they should do to modeling and showing people what they should be doing. Truth can only be told from within, so I began to live in my truth versus challenging people to live in theirs. That type of leadership is hard and it's rare, but it's real. It's real enough to keep me in it for the rest of my life because now the lessons will come from the leaps that I have taken in my life. The small idiosyncrasies will include things like daily meditation, becoming way more holistic and really consuming less. Consume less opinions from other people...their fears and their doubts because they'll cast them on you. Stay away from self-labeling because you limit yourself when you label yourself. Don't waste much time on small risk. I take big risk only now because I realize that those are the chapters that reveal the most to me. Those big risks allow me to jump knowing the net will appear.
The pressures in my journey are more or less from where I feel I could be versus where God is

directing me. It takes me having to just kill my ego.

At 30, you think that sleeping on a futon is the worst but in reality, being married to a woman that you barely love in a house that you really don't want to pay for; waking up to a job that you really hate is the worst feeling ever. The pressure has to be felt when I look and realize that a lot of people around me aren't living a life as fulfilled as mine but they're also able to have the comforts of life that I feel. That's where the meditation and the word of God come in. Your purpose is beyond you. It's beyond your comfort zone, it's beyond what you deem normal, and sometimes you have to go as far out in the jungle as you can to really see what God has for you. God will rebuild in the wilderness, but you have to learn how to be comfortable in the wild.

As I am in my hometown that I left to pursue myself 8 years ago and since leaving, I've seen the world. I've talked to the world. I found my voice. I found my sound. I've been on television. I wrote books but the beautiful thing about all of this is I am just now getting started. We as people need to understand that our purpose is so far beyond our potential and that we're capable of doin so many things that are going to amaze the world. However, the world will compliment your mediocrity but do not get caught up in that.

No matter how high you seek, God can always take you higher. It will not only keep you humble as it has me, it will keep you open. I cannot wait to see what's next, only because I cannot wait to share what I've seen. I truly believe that the truth we are seeing is the only bible some people are reading.

I am Corey Shane Taylor and I have survived PRESSURE.

Chapter 10

One of the most important aspects of life that many of us ignore is the well-being of our health. We will never be able to fully enjoy life and reach happiness at extreme levels if our health is unstable. The external things that we are marinating our minds with are killing us. The foods that we are consuming along with the exposure to drugs and mental health related issues are killing us as well.

Nowadays, it doesn't matter if you're rich, poor, educated or uneducated; poor overall health, drug abuse and mental health will defeat you if you allow it to.

Here in the news lately, we've been grimacing at headlines involving celebrities losing their lives to drug overdoses and many of them taking their lives...due to depression and anxiety. Celebrities aren't the only ones dealing with this issue...It's everywhere. Our close family and friends are suffering. It has gotten so bad that little kids are now showing up in the news. It was just in the news that recording artist, Mac Miller, lost his life to a drug overdose.

Pressure

In reading about the circumstances surrounding Mac's life, Mac said that he had enormous pressure growing up in the public eye.

> "A lot of times in my life, I've put this pressure to hold myself to the standard of whatever I thought I was supposed to be or how I was supposed to be perceived. And it created pressure." - Mac Miller

My favorite artist of all time, Michael Jackson, lost his life due to similar circumstances.

In our country, according to the Center for Disease Control, approximately 84 million American adults, more than one out of three have pre-diabetes. What's more shocking to me is that nine out of ten people with pre-diabetes...don't even know they have it. Obesity rates are reaching all-time highs and deaths from heart attacks and COPD are continuing to destroy our families.

How can we ever enjoy our fruits if we struggle taking care of ourselves? How can we fully maximize time spent with our family and friends if we're constantly back and forth in the emergency room or getting procedures done?

Have you ever had a family member pass away from an illness that was completely preventable? Have you ever had a family member die from an overdose or strung out on drugs so bad that you hardly knew who that person was? Have you yourself struggled with an illness and waited forever to go see a doctor? We as a culture have to shift our thinking in terms of taking care of ourselves and aspire to keep ourselves healthy.

My health is the most important responsibility in my life, right now. I can honestly say that I'm very fortunate because that hasn't always been the case. The difficult times that I've had with my body has forced me become more conscious. I watch what I eat. I exercise and stretch religiously. I drink more water and consume no alcohol. I've made it a point get my six to eight hours of sleep most nights.

My life has changed...I feel great!

Most people wait until something bad happens to them before they are ready to commit to a change. My opinion on that type of traditional mentality is to get out in front of the bad things that happen and avoid them if possible. There is no fun in being diagnosed with illnesses or being cut on by your doctors. There is no fun in physically not being able to participate in all life has to offer.

Speaking from experience!
I am in a space physically and mentally that I have never been in. I am experiencing joy in ways I never dreamt. I am mentally connected with myself in ways that I never imagined. I am starting to love myself more and more every single day. Even though I have five surgical scars on each one of my hips and a huge surgical scar that sits in the middle of my lower back, I physically feel and look better than I ever have.

I am starting to sleep well throughout the night and wake up every day refreshed and with a clear mind. I have become one of the best positive self-talkers in the world. I speak positivity to myself all throughout the day. I remind myself of how blessed I am and that God has me right where I need to be in life.

I remind myself to focus on me and not to worry about all the things that I can't control. I wake up five days a week and weight train at 4:30 a.m. in the morning. I hardly watch any Television. My Television has gone weeks without the power button seeing any action. I attend yoga classes several times a week and meditate daily. I have moved past the love for playing video games, the love for debating, the love of always being in competition with others and the love for social media, all which has resulted into me transforming into the person I am today.

An essential attribute that has also helped with my progression is having mentors. I have always struggled with trusting people and their intentions, so opening up to people has always been hard for me. However, once I developed the appreciation for constructive guidance and the openness of the opinions of others… I fell in love.

Corey Taylor, who you heard from in the previous chapter, is who I've looked up and talked to for spiritual guidance, inspiration, healthy living and mental wholeness. Corey has helped me from a holistic approach, tackle life with pure determination and confidence. There are also a few other people that I admire and have the opportunity of having positive relationships with as well. Each mentor that I have each bring something different to the table. I love gaining knowledge universally so that I become as well rounded as possible.

The only questions that I find myself repeatedly circling back to is why I waited so long to take my health serious. Why did I send my mental psyche through so much stress before? Why did I send my

Pressure

body through so much trauma before I realized how important my body was for my success? When you need assistance with having to be bathed...walked to the kitchen from the living room or assistance with getting yourself up from the couch...your perspective changes quickly.

I took it for granted that I was athletic enough to dunk a basketball with only taking one-step. I took it for granted that I could wake up, wash my face, brush my teeth and be out the door in seconds. Our bodies are our engines.

We can't accomplish anything if our engines don't work properly. I always say, treat your body like you do your car. Your car has a certain point to where it needs its oil changed. Our bodies do too.

I think half of the problem we face in society today, is people not loving themselves and measuring their success up with others.

We strive so hard to be like the next person that we think is doing great that we forget about our own greatness.

Everyone is on their own personal timeline with reaching success, so no time should go to waste comparing your life to theirs. Several of my college teammates left school early and became instant millionaires. They were the same people that I spent long days and nights with in the dorm as broke college students. It was easy for me to get down on myself because I didn't get that opportunity to become wealthy out of college, but I had to realize that I am still going to get there...just at another point and time in my life.

After having back surgery in 2013, I lost my first love, which was my ability to play basketball. I also lost my identity...self-esteem...self-confidence...my athletic figure...and myself.

From what I've learned to be depression, I started noticing the symptoms. I became very unhappy and lived constantly in a negative state of mind. I always wanted to be alone. I went periods without having an appetite. The world became a dark place. I wasn't quite sure how I would ever recover or if I would ever be who I once was.

I wasn't a nice person to be around. I often lashed out at those closest to me and as a result dissipated several relationships. Anytime anyone saw me and asked how I was doing, I pretended as if everything was ok just to avoid explanations. I kept a smile on my face to hide the pain. I felt alone in this fight. My pride wouldn't allow me to reach out for help. I figured no one would relate to what I was going through, so why reach out and make myself vulnerable.

I didn't know anyone in their early 20s that had experienced the type of trauma that I was suffering from, especially if they hadn't had their dreams taken away from them in an instant. There were not many people that I could turn to, so the pain stayed dormant.

My pops would tell me that I was suffering from depression and I always argued with him and denied his speculations. Who wanted to be labeled as the person who was suffering from depression? I had it made up in my mind that all this would go away as soon as my life had a purpose again. Looking back on that, I gambled with my life. Sometimes, fighting those types of battles alone doesn't always end well.

What if I never found my purpose, where do you think life would have taken me? For some people, the pressure would have been too immense and caused them to take their life down a path for the worst. This was during the time when I got heavily involved back in the church, and swallowed my pride of not sharing what I was going through. My pops became like my therapist. He and I would sit for hours while I flooded his ears with my emotions. He always seemed to have the answers. I always left him feeling better than when I came.

I did a lot of journaling and writing during the days that I saw the world as a dark place. Writing was very therapeutic. It gave me the ability to escape from the world and all of my problems.

I relived exciting moments throughout my life, as I would write them down. For example, the NBA had a lockout in 2011 and all of the top NBA superstars migrated to Lexington to play pick-up basketball with our team. I had the opportunity to play against the best players of this generation, LeBron James, Kevin Durant, Russel Westbrook and James Harden. The thoughts of having lived through experiences like that would bring me joy.

During the process of writing, I could sense a purpose for my life on the horizon and I knew that I could someday change lives by sharing my testimony.

I figure out so much about myself during these times. I came to the realization that success alone wasn't the recipe for joyfulness.

Pressure

After accomplishing a great deal in life and to still feel like something was missing left me confounded. I also had to realize that validation from others did nothing for me. Somebody else telling me how great of a person that I was served no purpose. I had to believe it in my heart that I was great.

I have grown to understand that success can also play against you with certain people. People struggle with the success of others. Our society is filled with unhappy people. What I had to understand was...people who aren't happy and miserable, don't know how to be happy for anyone else. Once I conditioned my mind to think that way, I started appreciating my success in ways I never have. I have accomplished some things that only God and I know about and I plan to keep it that way. I don't need the validation from others...NEITHER DO YOU.

Pressure made me who I am

Kyvin Goodin-Rogers

Growing up, I had dreams of playing D1 basketball, winning Conference Championships, National Championships, being drafted into the WNBA and helping my family get on their feet.

I have achieved some of these goals but not all of them. Which is one of the reasons that I went into depression. I was disappointed because I felt let down. I didn't know that I was in depression at first because I took Adderall, which helped me with my ADD, but also numbed majority of the pain because it kept me distracted from what I was really feeling.

During this time, I didn't really want to be around anybody. It was hard to be around people because I no longer trusted anyone. I felt like I didn't have a voice. I felt like every time that I would finally speak up, I would get shut down. I felt like I would never be able to accomplish the goals that I had for myself all because no one listened, which eventually began to hurt me physically and mentally.

I was too scared to seek help because of what I had already been through, so I decided that I could make it on my own. At least I was able to trust myself. I knew I would never let myself down, so I shut everyone else out. But at the same time, it was hard shutting people out because there's no one to talk to. I was to a point to where I would rather be lonely than hurt again.

Pressure

I didn't fully overcome depression until I met my coach at Union College, who taught me how to trust and love again. He taught me that people can be selfish in life, and you must be careful who you give your all to. He taught me that people would always let you down, but you can't let it define you. He told me to be the person that I never had.

I never knew how much your dreams could bring pain, but it hurts worst when no one listens to you.

when you feel like no one is listening, it leaves you in a dark place that's bitter, careless, feeling unwanted, worthless and ready to die. At one point, I can remember saying "God should've just taken me when I had my blood clot."

I had to learn that you can't identify yourself with the things in this world because they will always let you down.
For anyone dealing with depression, know that it's going to be okay. Don't be afraid to seek help; Somebody cares. Don't be ashamed that you are going through depression. You are not alone! Be gentle and compassionate with yourself, and know that better days are coming, but you must stay strong and be willing to fight your way out of depression. It's not easy but it'll be worth it.

Psalm: 34-17
The righteous cry out, and the Lord hears them; he delivers them from all their troubles.

I am Kyvin Goodin-Rogers and I have survived Pressure.

<u>Pressure made me who I am</u>

Katherine Hanly

As the mom of a teenage daughter, I am thankful that conversations around mental and physical health are starting to be more prevalent amongst the younger generations. Suicide rates in young kids and adults are continuing to soar. I think the biggest elephant in the room is finding the perfect solution. Will we ever?

The young children that I work with are mostly at-risk kids. In my line of work, I help and work with people who struggle with life crisis, addictions, self-discovery and many other things.

I have found that the majority of kids that I work with struggle with trusting and obeying authority. They struggle with bullying or being bullied. A lot of this can stem from a chaotic childhood, abusiveness, low economic levels, single parent households and traumatic experiences. I have also worked with kids whose parents were drug users and religiously fought in front of their children.

Every day is a struggle for people to manage their feelings and emotions. With all of the emotions and anger that these young kids are experiencing, I have noticed the commonality in self-harm. Kids are cutting themselves, taking opioids, drinking and committing suicide. Resources for physical harm are not quite as easy to access for the kids. A lot of them are afraid to speak up and ask for help. Many kids are afraid to ask for help, because they do not want to be made fun of or bullied. I have worked with young girls who have used sex to fill voids in their lives. They want to be liked, loved, and cared for. They don't have enough self-worth to love themselves and their own bodies, so they look for someone else to validate them.

I believe that we can overcome these pressures even though many have their doubts. There are many factors that will come into play with the paradigm being shifted, but I think it's possible. I think if we can get the people who are struggling with mental and physical health to concentrate on small things like exercising, meditation, positive self-talk, goal setting, asking for help, servicing others, living in the moment, and being happy with who you are, the paradigm will change. We also need more people servicing... reaching back to give a helping hand to those who need us.

    I am Katherine Hanly and I have survived PRESSURE.

<u>Pressure made me who I am</u>

Halle Simmons

As a teenager, it's a common emotion to feel helpless and to think that things will never end. You also have a lot of hormones amongst other things that are going on. The last several years, I have felt really depressed. I have high anxiety. I can't even begin to tell you why I go through these things. I haven't been able to figure out a cause. I think it's clinical and it is not a good feeling.

I always have zero motivation to do anything. I don't want to eat. I don't want to sleep. These emotions interfere with my day to day life because I'm usually an outgoing social person, but when I get hit by a depressive episode, I just shut down. I start to feel sad for no reason. I usually don't have very positive coping mechanisms. I will try to listen to music, go to sleep or watch videos on YouTube. I tried going to a therapist in the 6th grade, but then I stopped after a few weeks. Recently, I started with another therapist and that seems to be working a lot better this time around. I've been on medication for several months for depression, and recently have gotten on Anxiety medicine. I checked into a mental hospital because I didn't think that I was going to be able to stabilize myself. I needed the help.

My goal is for people to open up about the emotions their struggling with so that we can start saving lives. I want to help because I think mental health is something that needs to be talked about more. Kids struggle with opening up and asking for help because everyone feels so ashamed. I feel the same way at times.
Mental health is just as important as physical health. I've heard that you are more likely to die from suicide than a car crash. (New York Times).

I am Halle Simmons and I have survived PRESSURE.

Chapter 11

Around my junior year of college, I started forming a relationship with a close friend named Phillip Fowler. I always credit Phil for helping me with transforming my mind into wanting to be successful outside of sports, specifically in the business world. Phil and I organically started hanging out because we both had friends and family who were in the same circle. Phil would always challenge the athletes in our circle about gearing our minds towards ownership and having interest in starting businesses.

It's universally known that when athletes finish with their careers, the majority of them go broke or struggle with finding themselves. Phil didn't want to see that happen to anyone he had relationships with.

I was always interested in the type of conversations Phil frequently managed to bring up because owning my own businesses was something that flew onto my vision board throughout the years. I never had anyone to express those interests with. I didn't know anyone who had successfully run companies or anyone who had those interests. There were no lawyers who owned their own law firms, doctors who owned their own practices, investors, franchisees, or any type of businessmen around to inspire me.

Where I come from, we don't have these types of people as resources for us to reach out to and learn from. We're never taught to believe you can be anything other than an entertainer, NBA or NFL player. And, that's not counting those who are raised to believe that selling drugs can be another avenue of making yourself successful.

Phil is heavily involved in real estate and has his own consulting firm. In the past six years, I don't think there has been a day where Phil and I haven't spoken. Every morning I wake up or at some point during my day, I can count on getting some type of motivational text from Phil reminding me to keep chasing my dreams. There have been times where I was frustrated with things not coming to fruition as quickly as I wanted them to, and Phil has always been there keeping me focused on the end goal.

When you look at Phil's life from a far, he makes being an entrepreneur inspiring. He travels the world at his leisure, and has the freedom of time to do and go anywhere he wishes. I have joked with Phil on numerous occasions about wanting to live the life that he lives, but in all seriousness, we all should. But, some of us are never taught to be entrepreneurs and to strive for freedom of time. I most certainly didn't learn anything about entrepreneurship my entire academic career.

If you were fortunate to have any type of guidance around you at a young age, you were probably taught to get good grades, go to college and then join the work force. If you were taught to be self-sufficient, study the life of millionaires, network, and taught how to write business plans, then you were ahead of the curve.

That's the beauty of having a mind and a spirit that evolves. It's never too late to learn those types of things.

Pressure made me who I am

Phil Fowler

My environment was shaped by rational thoughts and critical thinking skills that I was taught at an early age. I was shaped by environment, and I believe that a lot of others are as well. I grew up in a house with educators. My mother is a retired teacher and my father has a background in education as an administrator. They were some of my biggest motivators and influencers. Your parents are your first teachers, so being able to learn from them helped me out tremendously.

As far as entrepreneurship, I grew up seeing my father own real estate and build property in several different states. I was able to see the process of my dad not only owning rental estate, but also the development stages of it. By experiencing all of this, I was able to develop a strong sense of how real estate worked, and I instantly felt passionate about it.

Naturally, I'm an educator and I love sharing the knowledge that I have organically with others. It's just who I am. I like helping others discover visions for themselves that they couldn't quite see. I have been close with several of Twany's family members for several decades, and when I got to know Twany, I noticed that he and I shared very similar characteristics. We come from different walks of life; however, we possess some of the same commonalities with many things. He has strong interpersonal skills much like I, and traits like those are recognizable when you first encounter people. It was easy to organically connect with Twany. Our relationship manifested into something bigger than probably he and I both expected. I've seen things in Twany that Twany hasn't seen in himself at times.

I encourage being an entrepreneur because you have the freedom to pursue your own limitless vision, and anything you're passionate about. It gives you an opportunity to create freedom of time if you create a system that works for you. And you can tailor your work according to whatever lifestyle you desire.

Being a successful entrepreneur forces you to be adaptive and if you're wise, you have the ability to unlearn and learn. One of the most rewarding aspects that I have personally achieved in being an entrepreneur is the ability to share my knowledge and what I've learned through all the highs and lows of entrepreneurship. Having the opportunity to execute and make your own vision come into fruition gives you an unexplainable joy that everyone who desires should also be able to experience.

I am Phil Fowler and I have survived PRESSURE.

I got my first experience of being an entrepreneur when I self-published my first book, *Full Court Press - Conquering Adversity Under Pressure.*

Writing a book was one of the hardest things I have ever done. It took an incredible amount of discipline and self-motivation. I had to hold myself accountable and stay dedicated to the process, because I was solely responsible for the completion and success of my book. It was very different from having teammates like I was accustomed to for so many years. I self-published, which was a huge risk in itself because every single penny needed to produce my product, came from my own pockets...much like first time business/company owners.

I wanted my book finished by the time I graduated college so that I could start my life outside of sports as an entrepreneur and change lives with my story. I applied a ton of pressure to myself because as with anything, I had my doubts.

What if no one likes the book and no one purchases it? What if my story isn't as impactful as I thought and I am never asked to speak? What if I waste thousands of dollars by writing this book? I had to train my mind to tell myself every day to not attach the success of my book with the number of sales, and to be happy with the product no matter what. When my thinking shifted, I loosened up and wrote more freely.

There was also the pressure of having to get everything done on my own. There was no coach to hold me accountable or anyone to hold my hand during the writing process. The entire writing process, editing, photo shoots, cover designing, amongst other things had to be done and done by me. Phil warned me before I jumped into the game that being an entrepreneur was extremely hard. I had times where I felt overwhelmed because my plate seemed too big but it was all part of the growing experience. I had to embrace it, especially, if I wanted my life to head down that road.

All of the advice Phil ever gave me was right. Being an entrepreneur was a cool life to live and experience. I was essentially my own boss and got to control my own time. I got to make all of my own rules and have final say with all decisions.

Putting my hands on the very first copy of my book was one of the best moments of my life.

I cried tears of joy; it didn't seem real.

It still shocks me that my face is on the front cover of a book that I published. What makes me extremely happy is that there are kids from my neighborhood that have reached out to me for advice on what it takes to write a book. Those kids now have a resource that I didn't have growing up…. someone to help them achieve something outside of the norm...someone who could show them that we can be entrepreneurs or authors if we choose. We don't always have to follow the norm and chase after entertainments and sports.

Once you experience success at something, you always get the urge to want more and sometimes even try different things. I know for myself, once I realized that I could be an entrepreneur and have success at it, I wanted to venture out into other things. What I found out very quickly is that entrepreneurship is not an easy career and it takes strong sacrifices in order to be successful. You have to be willing to take risks, but also accept that the risk could impact you negatively. Not all risk works out. Losing money is essentially one of the most dreadful consequences of taking a risk. My advice for taking a risk is being aware of all possible outcomes and doing your homework before you jump in head first. In business, never make decisions with your heart but with your mind.

I had to learn the hard way..........

I had a close family friend for over 20 years approach me about a business venture and it was disastrous from the moment I invested. The business idea was pretty good, but I didn't do my due diligence on the person that I was doing business with, and I lost money. I trusted the person because they were like family.

For the twenty plus years I had known the person, they had run multiple businesses and had all of the nicest things…big houses…cars… clothes etc. However, when I googled the person's name after the fact, I almost vomited at the headlines that popped up.

A mistake I will never make again. Lesson learned.

At that time, I was green as an entrepreneur and I allowed loyalty to cover up all the red flags.

That's the downside of being an entrepreneur that people rarely see. The failed businesses, the long nights, disagreements and the loss of large sums of money.

If you don't have a successful business or aren't making steady money, it will be hard to eat. That's where being an entrepreneur can become challenging. You have to be extremely disciplined. You may have to cut back on some of your spending habits, or spend less time doing things that inhibit you from working at your business. I have been working on writing this book for quite some time and I can't even tell you how many fun activities that I have passed up in order to focus on writing. I've missed fun trips with friends, and sometimes went months without hanging out so that my mind wouldn't lose sight of the goal.

Pressure made me who I am

Chris Hudson

When I was 10 years old, I started by selling candy in the neighborhood which led to me starting my own candy shop. The whole neighborhood would come over to buy candy from me. I also started selling yoyos to my classmates at school. Around that same time, my dad owned a cleaning service, where he cleaned commercial buildings and residential houses and he would let me work with him. When I would go to these residential houses, I would meet millionaires who were living in these huge houses, and every single person that I encountered was a business owner. Being able to be inspired by my dad, and then also meeting other successful people is what led me to want to get involved with entrepreneurship for myself.

This process for me started when I was 10 years old. That's when I was exposed to everything. The focus was about having the mindset and being able to tap into it.

Outside of my dad, I wasn't exposed to any other entrepreneurs in my community where I grew up. I'm from Lexington, Kentucky, and there were not a lot of successful clothing brands around. I was having a tough time trying to build something that I wasn't used to seeing and that made it hard because there wasn't anyone I could reach out to for help or guidance. The ones who were making money on their own accord were the guys who sold drugs, but I didn't want to follow in those foots steps. At that time, I got online and tapped into Myspace, and I was able to find a mentor by the name of Carl Wesley. He was based out of Texas. He had a clothing brand called 100 Figures. He was the first black entrepreneur that I had ever seen actually doing his own thing and being successful. He had celebrities, rappers and entertainers wearing his brand. I reached out to him for some guidance and help and he gave it to me. I befriended one other person who built the web layout for my brand. So, I had two inspirations, one who lived an hour away from me and one who lived on the other side of the country.

Pressure

The pressures with starting your own business for me was trying to make people believers. If you're creating something, you have to figure out a way to make people believe in what you're doing and why. With my clothing brand, Life's Journey, I wanted to create a design that I liked, but is likable to other people. I had to figure out how to go about marketing to people that will buy it. I didn't know what a target market was or understand how to go about reaching that target market. I was just creating T-shirts and selling them as I went. Many times, after I sold product to my friends and family, I would have so much product left over with no idea of what to do with it. It got to a point to where I had to give inventory away.

As I fought through all the pressure of starting my own company and now starting to see some success, I give all the glory to God. You Pray like it's on God and you grind like it's on you. I feel like I met God half way with my purpose and my vision, and now I can say that I am literally one connect away from the brand blowing up. To be able to have the influence to take something from the back of my trunk to all over the world is rewarding to see. I've put together fashion shows that attracted roughly 900 people, charity basketball events, and community events. To see a clothing brand that I started from scratch, starting to spread globally, has truly been a blessing.

For any of you who have aspirations of being an entrepreneur, the number one advice I would say is having that relationship with God is most important. Next is really trying to figure out what your purpose is. What happens a lot of the time is people are just living with no clue of who they are or with no sense of what they're supposed to be doing. Therefore, people end up wandering around working dead end jobs that they hate, but have to do in order to support themselves. In turn, a person ends up working 20-30 years at a job that they hate or they get comfortable in life and settle.

My advice to finding your purpose would be through prayer, purpose and exploring. If you're stuck within a routine of things, they become all you're accustomed to. Wake up, go to work, come home, and go to sleep, becomes a way of life for most people. People take the same route to work and the same route back to the house. It all becomes routine and people get comfortable. But, when you understand that you have a purpose on this earth, that's when you begin to change and inspire lives. People instantly become connected to you and depend on you to make it. They need your story. You also have to understand that life is going to be full of ups and downs. Throughout the process, the ups and downs are essentially the pieces that will help shape you throughout your journey. You may not understand it in the midst, but one day you will be able to look back on life and it will all make sense.

I am Chris Hudson and I have survived PRESSURE.

Chapter 12

When you were first introduced to religion, do you remember how you felt about it? Was it a family tradition to believe in what you believed in? Did you immediately develop a love and passion for it? How strong is your faith? Is maintaining your faith a huge pressure in your life?

In a life filled with so many up and down moments, I have never lost hope in my faith. My faith has been tested on many occasions and I've never thought about giving up on my faith.

When my grandmother first introduced me to the Church, I fell in love. I am almost 100 % sure that I love dressing in suits because of how my grandmother used to dress me for church. For years, there was this picture of me as a kid dressed in a suit with an enormous smile on my face that sat in my grandmother's living room. To this day, I take a picture of that picture every time I visit my grandmother's house. I always look at my face in that picture and meditate on how happy I looked as a kid. That innocent smile in that picture had no idea of what life was going to throw at me.

Pressure

As much disappointment and discontent that I had experienced along my journey, and at thirty years old to have a smile on my face like I did in that picture is extraordinary to me.

When I developed a foundation that was hell bent on believing in God and relying on my faith to get me through tough times, I didn't fully understand what that meant. It wasn't until I really started to experience the pressures of life that I fully had a grasp on what type of commitment it took to stay loyal to your faith. I have survived solely on the "everything happens for a reason," conviction. Seriously, I have said that to myself over a million times. Every time something happens, good or bad, I will say that to myself and move on from the situation. Now, there have been occasions where I questioned myself at times and the possibility of certain things happening to me, but my faith always centered me.

For the first time in my life, I am experiencing real JOY. I am experiencing what life is like to be fully content and happy with the life that God has provided for me. My appreciation for certain things is elevated and I don't take a day on this earth for granted. I have reached a point in life where people's opinions are irrelevant. Societal values are inapplicable. And, nothing matters except my inner peace.

Years ago, if you would have asked me what it would have taken for me to reach this point in my life, I would have depicted a much different visual. Materialistic desires and pleasures would have been my foundation along with basing my success on what I could or could not do for other people.

Early on in my life, it was easy to question why I was born into certain situations or why I had to be dealt the cards that I received. It was easy to question why I had to lose a close cousin, a best friend and several others to gun violence. It was easy to question why I had to suffer career-ending injuries and be forced to walk away from the precious game of basketball that I loved with everything in me... all the way down to my soul. It was easy to question those things.

In my mind, I was the chosen one. I was the savior. I was the protector. I was the one gifted with all of the talent to make it big in sports. Why didn't it work out for me?

Now I realize, it did work out for me. I am the chosen one. I am the savior. I am the protector. I did make it big……. JUST NOT IN SPORTS

Pressure

God blessed me with an abundance of talent and used sports as a vehicle to drive me right to this specific point in life where I currently am. Sports and the injuries I endured gave me a story. They tested my faith. They gave me a voice. They gave me a purpose. Sports will never last forever but my faith will.

Acknowledgements

I wanted to dedicate this section of my book to give thanks to my Lord and Savior, Jesus Christ, for giving me life and planting the faith seed in me from the very beginning. At every turn and every storm, I know God was right there with me, giving me the strength and the faith to believe in him, knowing that I would be standing tall at the end of road. To the wonderful people that have impacted my life in many ways, I thank God for sending you. I thank God for giving you the strength to be there for me during times of struggle and times of celebration.

In 2015, when Rev. Willis Polk re-baptized me at the Imani Christian Church in Lexington, Kentucky, I washed away every sorrow and re-confessed my love for Jesus Christ. I was ready to walk in newness with God because in the previous twenty-six years of my life, God showed me exactly who he truly was. He showed me that he was a God that will never leave us nor forsake us. And, for that, I will forever be Joyful.

Also, I sincerely from the bottom of my heart want to thank you for taking the time to connect with me and the many others throughout this book to see us through the pressures that we have lived and survived. Us connecting was no mistake because God doesn't make any!!!!

Rev. Willis G. Polk, I, Senior Pastor of the Imani Baptist Church, Lexington, Kentucky.

I truly count this invitation from Brother Twany Beckham, as a huge honor and a great blessing, to help him close out this publication on such a very personal note. Matter of fact, he felt he would be remiss if he failed to include this very personal matter.

When I first met Twany Beckham, a few years back, I met who I thought to be a very shy young man. But my personality would not allow it to be that way. And, we have since become great friends.

Twany has shared with me, on many occasions, many details of his life all the way back to his childhood. That reflection makes it easy for me to help him publish this statement concerning what has become a dominate awareness in his life. This awareness is also a force and a guide for him, a very presence in all that he does.

What Twany possesses, he realizes was first established as a result of his grandmother's invitation to him to attend church with her when he was a kid. Twany says, "Immediately I fell in love with that introduction to the church and to church life." He said, "I loved not only the House of Faith and the Life of Faith so much, I can remember loving to dress up to go there".

Un-be-knowing to Twany, that experience would prove to be a constant characteristic of this consciousness. In his books and in his speeches, you hear him say, "my faith, my faith, my faith has always been there." He will say, "It has carried me and has not failed me".

In the bible in II Timothy chapter 1:3-6, the Apostle Paul referred to the same experience in the life of young Timothy. Timothy was facing great challenges as a young fellow in his work. The challenges were of such that it would make anyone give up and drop out of the race. Twany, like Timothy, has detailed for us his many, many challenges. Life can be hard and can get hard. But thanks be to God that there is a something we can depend on in life to get us through.

Paul said to Timothy at such a time, "I call to remembrance the unfeigned faith that is in thee, which dwelt first in thy grandmother, Lois." Paul said, "I am persuaded that it is in thee also. Therefore, I put thou in remembrance that you stir up that gift of God, which is in thee".

It is this gift that has helped Twany in the face of many, many challenges from the early days of his childhood, even to this very day. In his early childhood, it was that gift that enabled him to raise the right questions about poverty, no father in the home, tough neighborhoods and bad influences. The gift helped him come down on the right side of those experiences that causes him to be alive today. The gift has kept him sane and safe. It kept him, especially when he saw that his basketball aspirations were cut way short, to not be bitter but helped him be better.

It is clear to Twany Beckham that this transcendental conscious is becoming more and more dominate in his life as the years come and go. I know, as the bible says, his eyes have not seen and his ears have not heard what the Lord has in store for him.

I think that what he has is a great possession for anyone to be able to acknowledge and embrace, especially at the age of thirty.

May he continue.

Interlude Three

Kobe Bryant interview with Rich Eisen

Eisen: Now that your basketball career is over Kobe, and when it all comes down to it, you want to do what with your second career, Kobe?

Kobe: I want to be able to use sports as the greatest metaphor for life. We feel like if we can teach kids how to deal with anxiety, how to deal with pressure, how to deal with failure, how to deal with success, through sports, I believe it helps them become better people. If your kid is struggling with something like a bully at school or struggling with the pressure of taking tests because it's just too much, how do you practice that? As a father, you can go to your daughter and say, "Work your hardest, don't worry about the end result," but those are just words. They have to physically and emotionally put themselves in that same situation over and over to really understand how to deal with it. Sports do that for you. So now, through sports, when you practice every day and compete in games, you have these emotional challenges and you get used to figuring out how to navigate yourself through. Which in return, helps you figure out how to become a better test taker and vice versa.

Inky Johnson – YouTube video

As long as I can attack things with the mentality of not me but us; as long as I can attack things and dismantle my ego and my pride when I don't get what I want. I understand the purpose of what we're all working for is a lot greater than individual accolades. As long as I can attack it with the right mentality, the opposition, the adversity, the challenge and the association of it will be very different. When I hit something that can crush me, I will look at it and associate it with growth instead of pain. It's not like every day I wake up and say adversity come and see me but when it comes, I don't view it as why do I have to go through this but when I get through it, it's an incredible opportunity for me to grow. When I get through it, I'm going to be a better father because of it. When I get through it, I'm going to be a better teammate because of it. I've had every opportunity to stop and quit. I've looked in the face of the opposition and said it would be disrespectful because of what I've made a vow to. It wasn't in my life contract. It wasn't in my life contract to quit when I didn't get what I wanted. It wasn't in my life contract to stop because the deal didn't turn out the way that I thought that it would turn out. It wasn't in my life contract when uncertainty hit, for me to step back and say you know what man, I give up. IT WASN'T IN MY LIFE CONTRACT!

Remember at the beginning of this book when I told you that PRESSURE can kill??? As you can see...PRESSURE can also make you the strongest individual on the planet. Pressure has given me the courage to share my story with many around the world!!

Twany spreading the truth about PRESSURE!

Pressure

After winning a NCAA National Championship, graduating from college and Authoring two books, I was back at the place where it all started…the basketball courts in Beecher Terrace Projects- in Louisville, Kentucky. As I was posing for this picture, buildings in the place I once called home were getting bulldozed to the ground, literally. They are tearing down and doing away with the Beecher Terrace Community. This was such a surreal feeling and moment for me. The place I once called home, and the place a kid like me was never supposed to make it out of, was back and ready to throw away all the illusions. I've beaten the odds and am here to let everyone in the world know that you can beat the odds too and it doesn't matter where you come from.

Pressure

Twany Beckham

Contact me:

Email - Tbeckham11@yahoo.com
Website - twanybeckham.com

@TwanyBeckham11

@twanybeckham

@twanybeckham

Twany Beckham

Made in the USA
Middletown, DE
27 November 2018